ASTROLOGY IN MESOPOTAMIAN CULTURE

ASTROLOGY IN MESOPOTAMIAN CULTURE

AN ESSAY

BY

A. E. THIERENS
Author of Natural Philosophy, Elements of Esoteric Astrology and General Book of the Tarot

WITH 2 FIGURES

WIPF & STOCK · Eugene, Oregon

Wipf and Stock Publishers
199 W 8th Ave, Suite 3
Eugene, OR 97401

Astrology in Mesopotamian Culture
By Thierens, A. E.
Softcover ISBN-13: 978-1-7252-7930-8
Publication date 4/29/2020
Previously published by Brill, 1935

To the memory of the late
Rev. Prof. Dr. ALFRED JEREMIAS
who taught us and demonstrated the necessity for learning the language of the Mythos, in order to understand it, this humble work is dedicated.

CONTENTS

On the 11th of January 1935 the Reverend Professor ALFRED JEREMIAS, *D.D., PH.D., passed away at Leipzig. I consider it a worthy memorial in honour of him that in this same year the present essay will be published by one to some extent congenial to him. Because notwithstanding all objections and hesitations the history of the Religion of Ancient Babylonia and Assyria owes a great debt of gratitude to ingenious historians like the late* HUGO WINCKLER *and to theologians like the deplored* ALFRED JEREMIAS.

We welcome now this exposition of the ancient Babylonian view of the world on an astrological basis. Mr A. E. THIERENS *is a natural philosopher who speaks as representative of a cosmical conception which is fundamentally identical with that of the ancient Mesopotamian astrologers themselves. We hope many will take an interest in his effort to come to an understanding of the cosmic wisdom of the Chaldeans and of their predecessors in ancient Mesopotamia. Still his method and his conclusions in the sphere of occult sciences are on his own responsibility.*

Noordwijk near Leyden FRANZ M. TH. BÖHL
1935, July 15th

I. INTRODUCTION

When I had studied astrology during about 30 years I had heard a good many hints at the Assyrio-Babylonian culture as being the astrological period in the history of mankind *par excellence*. Hints it were, not divulging much exact knowledge about this period.

Realising that the majority of astrological authors did never study this period themselves, I felt the necessity for a particular notion of it as unavoidable and even inexorable. My first step in this direction immediately made me meet with the amiable and courteous help of Dr. F. M. Th. Böhl, Professor of Assyriology at Leyden. A three years' study in his library guided by the valuable indications of the owner himself brought me the desired information. At least as much of it as I wanted and was able to gather. My hearty thanks to Prof. Böhl must be expressed here. I may not forget adding how I am well aware that my shortcomings and even more so my conclusions are not in the least covered by the responsibility of my learned host. I beg the reader to bear this in mind as well.

As to the exact knowledge and the sources in which it was found, the stupendous work done by Assyriologists — historians as well as philologists — became a revelation to me, the first thing revealed being the length of the period covered by Mesopotamian culture with its astrological characteristic; the second being the mass of material found out.

Owing to the length of the historical period, which reaches as far back as about (before) 3000 b.C., we must expect gradual changes in the belief of the people as well as in the mysticism of the priestly class. Therefore it will be almost impossible to arrive at a conviction, which should hold good for the length of the whole period of about 3000 years. We find also changes of language being the cause of changes in names given and surnames addicted to the planets, stars and zodiacal signs.

An almost perfect guide through the vast domain of literature here is the volume of Conrad Bursian's *Jahresbericht über die Fortschritte der klassischen Altertums-Wissenschaft* (243. Band, Jahrgang 1934), in which astronomy and astrology, astral religion and astral mythology are treated by Wilhelm Gundel. The most important part of it contains astronomy and astrology by the Babylonians (Chapter VIII).

As to the astronomical foundations — scarce at the beginning of these 3000 years, manifold since King Ashurbanipal of Assyria founded his renowned library of copied ancient cuneiform tablets — the enormous work of Father F. X. Kugler S. J., together with the investigations of Thureau Dangin, Boissier, Thompson, Virolleaud and Weidner, leads to respectful admiration, which is not diminished by the fact that many words in this language appear to have different meanings or interpretations and moreover the whole of it appears to be written in different languages, as different as Semitic (Accadian) and northern (Sumerian) origins possibly can be.

The narrow contact in which Babylonians and Assyrians were brought by history with Israelites of course accounted for the great interest put into the just awakening archeology of this Mesopotamian culture about 1875 and 1900, when G. Smith wrote his *Chaldean Account of Genesis* and when Fr. Delitzsch wrote his essays on *Babel und Bibel*. Exaggeration of the importance led to the name of Pan-Babylonism, which ascribed to Mesopotamia the keynote of theological knowledge on an astrological basis, a statement strongly contradicted by others. It was the suggestion that every item and figure in the Bible was to be found in Babylonia already, which roused a good many opponents. Together with Friedrich Delitzsch, Peter Jensen, Hugo Winckler and Alfred Jeremias were reckoned to be the principle Pan-Babylonists, the late Father Kugler figurated as the first and most powerful of their opponents among which is further to be counted Hugo Gressmann. The Ancient Orient became an object of strife and in the series *Im Kampfe um den Alten Orient* Jeremias and Winckler carried their arguments in defense of their views. When the former arrived at conclusions based on legends and myths, Father Kugler could not refrain from calling their 'symbolic explanation' only 'a dreamlike construction'[1]) (IBB, p. 44/45). Pan-Babylonists explained a certain meaning of the Gilgamesh Epic, one of the most renowned legends, by taking Gilgamesh in a symbolic way, on occount of his nature being said 'two-thirds divine'. Father Kugler answered that you could as well call Lewis IX of France a symbolic being. He wrote a satirical narrative of the *'memoires du Sire de Joinville'* (*Ein Mahnwort und ein Exempel*, IBB). He criticises the assimilation introduced by the other party of the biblical Esther and Mardochai with Ishar and Marduk of the Babylonians, asking finally: "Does this mean really that our Esther-book not only has a historical but even a mythological background? In no way!" (*Zur Aufklärung. — Ueber die Sternenfahrt des Gilgamesch*).

One cannot escape from the idea of Father Kugler being afraid of a too far stretching symbolism making its appearance, finally threatening to destroy biblical, perhaps New-Testamental figures. Still he has probably been carrying his opposition and renunciation too far and was taken to task by Ernest Weidner, who ends his considerations thus: "I judge it unnecessary to spill another word on the conclusion *Ein Mahnwort und ein Exempel*" (pag. 15 of his recension of Kugler's IBB in KAO 1913).

Gundel calls the criticism by Gressmann and Rühle matter of fact and sober. Nevertheless it is answered by Jeremias (*Zur Frage des Pan-Babylonismus*, pag. 3) by saying not incorrectly: "It is as if an anatomist would say that he had searched the nightingale but found no voice; incapability to understand the language of the mythos being no reason for reproach, as little as the fact of lacking musicality. The unmusical however doesn't write recensions on music". Jeremias himself gave the following definition: "Pan-Babylonism — the unlucky word came from our opponents, he says — points out the doctrine of a pre-existing harmony between heavenly and earthy happenings, from which were derived *e.g.* the motives of the Saveour-mythos, and which doctrine must have travelled through the world in the course of time. 'Babylonian' is the doctrine apparently in so far as it pre-supposes a native country in which astronomy was the foundation of the culture, which was actually the case in Babylonia ('chaldean wisdom'). If another country could be proved to be as well a source in the same way (the group of Hüsing speaks of an 'arian system') it would not alter the fact..." (Theol. Lit. Zeitung 1911, p. 3 *Zur Frage des Pan-Babylonismus*).

The culmination of the struggle for and against Pan-Babylonism is probably passed and certainly other countries in the world have yielded evidence of cosmic foundations for their theological systems and culture — China, Peru, *e.g.* — but as to Babylonia the question remains: are we justified in looking on legends and myths as symbolical and containing a spiritual and moral meaning on account of their symbolical significances — or not.

There is the life of the people, and a grand culture speaking from these documents evidently. There is another thing to be had from these sources investigated than historical and philological items only. Behind them is the life of the spirit and soul itself. Theology and even cosmology lies at the root: it is cosmic life itself, penetrating peoples and cultures and being manifested in myths and legends and holy scriptures. As far as we are able to see, this is the proper meaning of what has been wrongly called Pan-Babylonism.

My research wat not an investigation of the sources, but of the contents as rendered by men of the Faculty. Philology and history went before. Astrology was to be investigated afterwards. Assyriology in the linguistic and historical line has been developed too far to ask either criticism or corroboration of a humble student of astrology.

Instead of quotations in the original language I have translated all into english, even in cases where an English translation existed. Quotation-marks are mostly omitted, though the contents are given as literally as possible.

Concluding: there are two different elements in this essay, *viz.* 1⁰ the scientific

[1]) "...*eine traumhafte Kombination*"...

sources and quotations and 2^{0} some conclusions and astrological conjectures in which I have indulged. I can only hope that I may have succeeded in making clear the difference between these two in every case, but above all that the spiritual or deeper meaning of the generally accepted astrological foundations of this Mesopotamian culture will become more evident.

II. ORIENTATION

Considering the remarkable position of astrology with regard to the present period of civilisation, the first question which arises is this: how did astrology arrive here? — an organic relation with our university is wanting: presentday academical science, philosophy and theology ignore astrology. It exists, but it stands apart. It was chiefly introduced or re-presented by theosophists; or at least it came to us along theosophical lines. Still — and this is the second question — do we not meet with symptoms and even with a marked literature of the subject in every century? Indeed. — Has astrology ever disappeared finally and totally? — The answer must be: no. Never during the last five or six thousand years of historical times — this includes the periods of Egyptian, Sumerian, Babylonian, Indian, Chinese, Greek and Roman culture — has there been one age in which signs and symptoms of astrological principles and ideas were missing, nor even the distinct study of the same.

The place which astrology occupied during the subsequent ages of christian culture among the peoples which were its confessors, has been gradually diminished in importance and since the rationalistic movement and *culte de la raison* of the eighteenth century, the ultra-aristotelian materialism in science culminating in the nineteenth century, it has been perfectly backed out from the scene. Not only this, but there remained no logical relation between astrology and the preponderant sciences. Academical people are quite at a loss, what to make out of this 'funny' ancient lore, to which they appear unable to find any access.

The beginning of this gulf between astrology and academical science lies earlier than our days. Kepler already in his time appeared to have felt a shyness in coming to the front as its exponent: he apologizes for his courting the silly daughter (astrology) for the sake of earning the favours of the very learned mother (astronomy) — a weakness, which we may readily forgive him, when we understand how much he was pressed by his economical miseries, but which remained a weapon in the hands of the opponents of astrology during ages afterwards, because it demonstrated the suspectness of astrology even in Kepler's days. — Still Kepler's saying is chronologically incorrect in so far as astrology appears to be the elder of the two, astronomy coming to be realised and worked out geometrically only very much later. Alfred Jeremias put it in a concise saying *i. e.* that the heavens, to the ancient Mesopotamians, were first only a picturebook, a cipheringbook afterwards (HAOG p. 202 and 244).

The great philosopher Hegel gives a specimen of the way in which astrology was judged at the beginning of the 19th century, where he writes: „the contents of astrology must be rejected as a superstition".

During the last decennia of the 19th and the beginning of the 20th century, however, new insights are growing gradually, opening a new era with regard to old lore and ‚superstition'.

Thus Franz Boll in his remarkable work *Sphaera:* Astrology after its origin is not a superstition, but the expression or sediment of a religion or world-vision of imposing totality – which was said after Hugo Winckler's researches and Delitzsch' *Babel und Bibel.*

Within an age after Hegel we came to conclusions remarkably different. In the course of a lecture on ancient astronomical observations Boll said in 1917: The vulgar working of miracles remains for ever show and unsatisfactory. — Astrology, which we cannot dismiss with the general nomer of 'superstition', is of an other sort. — It contains a striving after a grand world-conception as an impulse and as fruit at the same time in itself.

Bouché Leclercq, the author of *L'Astrologie Grecque*, speaks of astrology as if it only deserved ridiculising as a stupid superstition, but he was called to order by Martin Knapp in a commentary on the said work: The sentence (p. XVI of the *Bibliographie*) 'the study of astrology has nothing to expect, I think, neither of archeology, nor of numismathics, nor of epigraphy' speaks for itself. He who approaches the riddle of the sphinx in astrology in a spiritual attitude like this, has very little chance to reach any deeper knowledge.

Again we find this remarkable qualification of astrology by Boll on the 49th Congress of Philologists at Basle as a 'grand effort at a universal world-conception after laws of nature which may be misunderstood but which are inexorable' — and we come to conceive that the scientists, who searched the ancient orient, brought us a considerable step nearer to the reunion of astrology and the more official sciences.

There is more in it than sheer recognition of astrology as a 'science' by the academical faculties. On the other hand it is more than flattering the vanity of astrologers — albeit that personal vanities of people considering themselves as such may perhaps be at stake. There is a more important side to it than the favour of the official representatives of those faculties. The better amongst them are even not at all inaccessible to objective considerations about astrology. The question lies in a re-union of the different faculties of human cognition and the rediscovering of certain laws of nature, which were more or less veiled to our vision during the last centuries, by the fact that other laws of nature came more to the fore and drew our attention above all, *e.g.* Physics, with its theories about atoms, electrons, vibrations and waves; Technics, with its problems of commercial value; Astronomy, and Sociology. At the same time the said academical sciences have built on this shore the pillars which may once carry a bridge between it and yonder shore, where astrology and occultism in general have theirs ready and are waiting. The very important results of archeology, in particular those of the near East on the plain of the Euphrates and Tigris, add weight to these pillars and are carrying materials for the bridge.

It has become a commonplace to call 'the Chaldeans' the proper or original representatives of astrological culture and science, the historical godfathers of astrology. Gradually by archæological researches it became more and more evident how important the spiritual and psychological background of the astrological element in the civilisation of the mesopotamian peoples was. In one of his last puplications, *Der Kosmos von Sumer* (introduction), Alfred Jeremias says: "The sumerian problem shews itself more and more as the most important among all problems of spiritual history of mankind. In Sumer I see the line of culmination within the formations of high-culture which came into existence towards the end of the younger stone-period about 3500 b.C. in these regions of paradises on earth. The Herman-Wirth-society spreads the ideas, from Germany, that in the sunken Arctis-Atlantis a still older high-culture existed. I leave alone explanations with this thesis. In only wish to show the following points:

In Arctis-Atlantis there must have been a teaching containing:

— the source of the oldest and purest faith: the direct vision;
— One God and the saying purely spiritual without any personification or materialisation;
— the way of God after the course of aeons (the course of the year);
— the same as the root of symbolism;
— in the centre: the One Madonna as the Mother of the Child-Redeemer, the Saviour, in whom God and Man are one.

As far as I see Herman Wirth has not said that this actually is the *original teaching of Sumer*, as I have demonstrated in my *Handbuch der Altorientalischen Geisteskultur*."

The ario-germanic sympathies of Herman Wirth may have prejudiced more or less towards the ario-germanic source of civilisation, but we must expect certainly, that neither the latter, nor Mesopotamia, were te only sources of astrological influences of foundations in civilisation. The light of archaeological researches is well directed towards the plain of Euphrates en Tigris nowadays, but this does not contradict important indications in finds of old civilisatons in Egypt, India, China, Mexico, Peru, containing astrological features, which justified or even compelled to the conclusion, that astrology was part of it as a whole.

It is primarily along the line of symbolism, that we must expect proof or at least indications of it. More has been engraved in stone than even papyrus-leaf or bark could preserve for posterity. In simple symbols much more was said than in extensive descriptions. Compare Goblet d'Alviella and Churchward. Moreover we may point at the *Surya Siddhanta,* the *Brihat Samhita* and *Brihat Jataka* of Hindu literature, the Egyptian *Book of the Dead* and so many other works in the growing lists archaeological literature; the matter of symbolism certainly deserving special attention and a volume apart.

A good many years more of researches will probably be wanted before present-day humanity will definitely be standing before the clear conception of the common cosmological ground, lying — or at least suspected — behind the different religious and cultural visions of life, which ruled the periods of highest civilisation.

Let us define what we have to understand by an 'astrological' type of culture. A pantheon with the accompanying speculations on the qualities and principles of gods and goddesses is to be found within almost every great civilisation. In this respect they all might be called more or less cosmological. The astrological type, however, appears only there where these cosmic forces or principles are supposed to be the qualities of certain constellations, surrounding our solar system, and of the Sun, the Moon and the planets belonging to the latter. They appear in such a case as motoric forces ruling the life on earth. Constellations as well as Sun, Moon and planets are then to be regarded as the houses, embodiments or vehicles of cosmic forces mentioned; their ruling and governing of the life on earth appears in every instance as the work of a divine world.

The remarkable fact is that in the mesopotamian civilisation we are not able to indicate the moment when astrology proper came up, nor the *auctor intellectualis* who forged this astrological link. We cannot prove when and where the cosmological conceptions are beginning to bear the type of 'astral mythology'.

It was in the time of Gudea that a tale existed in which the goddess *Ninâ* or *Nanshe,* daughter of *En-ki*, an earthy goddess of the water, figured and also her 'sister' *Nisaba*, a profetess, who carries the 'table of the good star', appearing in a dream to Gudea (Gudea Cyl. A. V. 13ff.). This — says Kugler — was 'the first appearance of any astrology in Mesopotamia' (SSB, p. 136 Book II, 1909). Gudea ruled about 2320 b.C. — Well, if not astrology, it has been at least a symptom of an existing belief in it.

It will be even very difficult, if not impossible, at the present stage of the astrological researches in different parts of the world, to explain with some chance of accuracy who were the original carriers of the astrological vision of life, properly speaking. In the low countries of the Euphrates and the Tigris several elements have been mingled, peoples coming from different races. As this remains a subject of thorough historical investigations, we shall abstain here from conclusions, waiting for further results. Certain is that an older layer of population was mixed with the influx of a people, that has been called sumerian, and which perhaps, just as the Hittites in Asia Minor came from the North; on the other hand mixed with several and subsequent semitic imigrations, descending from the Arabic Plateau: Akkadians, Amorites, Aramaeans, Arabs. From an other side came Elamites and Kassites, from the North-East and East.

The Sumerians are the principal but not the oldest group; in Western Mesopotamia another important group was that of the Churrites, which were present in the plain perhaps before the Sumerians.

If the origin of the Sumerians is to be considered as proto-arian, then Herman Wirth would have some evidence on his side in deducting the astrological features of Mesopotamia from a nothern culture. A general conviction for the latter is missing, because even a shadow of proof is wanting, after the opinion of a good many of the most important and learned investigators.

So we are not able to point out where the original astrological thread has been spun in.

In the fertile but narrow plain of the two rivers there have probably been three distinct international periods, as far as the present standpoint of science goes: the first may have been that marked by the entry of the Sumerians about 3600 b.C.; the second containing the time, which has been generally given the name of El-Amarna-period, during which in Egypt the 18th and 19th dynasties ruled, and a very characteristic relation existed between this country and the assyrio-babylonian culture about 1400—1300 b.C.; the third having been called the hellenistic period, in which Greeks and later still the graeco-roman culture laid contacts with Mesopotamia and still farther East. Then the last fruit of mesopotamian civilisation was carried by the people of 'Chaldea', around the Mediterranean, and handed to the rest of Europe under the name of 'chaldean lore' — to come after the Middle-Ages to a slow and unglorious death — apparently at least.

When in later ages we hear the name 'Chaldeans' called as the godfathers of astrology aud reprensentatives of mesopotamian culture, we must imagine them in no way as the originators of the science, nor of te culture, but only bearing the name of the last mesopotamian dynasty ruling Babylon, of which Nabopolassar was the founder and the first king coming to the throne in 625 b.C. During the next or hellenistic period the reflex of Babylon upon graeco-roman culture spread under the name of the Chaldeans, because the Greeks and Romans and other peoples of that period had known the Chaldean dynasty only and knew relatively very little of former millennia.

By its nature astrology was a vision of life and a religion all from the beginning and *de facto* belonging to a period of civilisation, extending over at least 4000 years. The constancy of the fundamental elements in this culture, which certainly deserve our admiration and attention, may perhaps *a priori* count as significant with regard to the importance and vitality of the same — heavenly — foundations. If not a proof, at least an indication.

The powerful influence of mesopotamian or babylonian civilisation, which has been bearing during so many centuries this astrological vision of life, was indicated by Dr. F. M. Th. Böhl in his dissertation *Kanaanäer und Hebräer*, where he states that the babylonian language was used for diplomatic service in all Lesser Asia and up to Egypt, the same as Latin was in use all over Europe afterwards. This is a *syncretism*, afterwards converted into Hellenism.

Böhl wrote in the said dissertation: The great merit of Hugo Winckler will remain, that he has clearly worked out an important element of the antique worldconception in the formula '*Himmelsbild ist Weltenbild*', macrocosm is microcosm once more. He used the expression '*Entsprechungstheorie*' — theory of analogy or correspondence, we could translate it perhaps in English. The configuration of the heavenly bodies appears not only as an example, it is clearly a construction of immediately inducing forces as well, by which cycles and cyclic happenings are caused, which are repeated in the happenings on earth. The doctrine of cycles is one of the most preponderant parts of the whole theory (p. 99).

The question has been put and contested whether the praecession of the equinoxes has been known early in Mesopotamia or whether it was observed only late and not before hellenistic times. This cycle, as we know, means the retrograde movement of the equinoxes trough the constellations of the zodiacal belt in the heavens, which takes about 25900 years. It has been called sometimes the World-Year, or Platonic-Year, and constituted together with the year-, month-, day-cycles on earth very principal foundations of this astrological world-conception. Of ultimate importance is "this grand fundamental idea of the inner analogy of the harmony of the cosmos in space (configuration of heaven and earth) and time (calendar and cyclic movement)..." (Böhl *op. cit.* p. 99). It is this idea, which we note as typical for mesopotamian culture principally represented by the Babylonians in their centre of civilisation, science and theology.

We will not enter here upon the fact that the contemplation of the heavens by the Babylonians — let us take this name for the whole of the peoples under this civilisation and world-conception — led to errors, sinning against logic thought, *e.g.*

the *post hoc ergo propter hoc, i.e.* the supposition as if a succession in time were the real cause of subsequent conditions in facts following each-other in the same way; the question if one has the right to speak of an *Analogie-zauber* (analogy-spell) with the accent strongly upon the last word, indicating the meaning of worthlessness and rejection. Let us see what history teaches and what documents are able to prove.

The doctrine of correspondences is indeed the principal thing. Not only that the earth was viewed as an image of the heavens, but the idea is carried further on and private life is considered to be a reflection of the king's life and the latter as that of the life of the gods; the microcosm as a clockwork, that is following the macrocosmic constellations *per analogy*[1]).

This is a grand conception and, like in everyone of the really great periods of civilisation, we must expect, this people lives religious and in an overwhelming state of consciousness of its gods in daily life. More and more names of gods were taken over and carried by kings and priest-princes — which may have been considered to be gods themselves, or his representatives — and even by high functionaries and dignitaries, who all of them appeared to have been conscious to bear as it were a divine responsibility. Every town stands under the protecting dominion of one of the gods. Thus we find the sumerian town Eridu under the rule of Ea, god of the sea and the water; Ur in particular under that of Sin (the Moon). In Borsippa rules Nebo (Mercury) and in Babylon the great god Marduk (Jupiter) as the mighty protector of the king and the people for some 2000 years; the capital of the Assyrians carries the name of Assur after the martial and solar god Ashur, while Ninivé was devoted to Ishtar (Isis or Venus).

In his *Handbuch der Babylonischen Astronomie* Weidner opens his introduction with:

Astronomy and astrology — two unseparable ideas in ancient Babylonia. Never and nowhere on their foundation a world-conception has been built of so gigantic a unity as here. World-conception and conception of the heavens are one — no system can posses a fundamental formula which is more clear and at the same time all-containing. The priest who offered prayers to the star-gods, had to acquire a concise knowledge of the starry sky, he had to study the movements of the heavenly bodies and their mutual places for the sake of the deity. In this way in the days of old the first astronomical science came into existence, but at the same time the secondary trade of astronomy, star-lore, go to an important significance. In the service of religion both interwoven came to an marvellous growth in Babylonia; thence they spread over all peoples of antiquity, nay even after their Middle-ages far over the world and up to America. The astronomical knowledge of the Babylonians remained unsurpassed until the times of the european Middle-ages; no people of antiquity knew so much of the stars as they did. When in their later ages the disciples of babylonian astronomers got the permission to call themselves Chaldeans, it was held in high esteem in Rome. Up to the time of the (european-Th.) Middle-ages the babylonian astrology has kept its foothold ominiously. Even at present there are remains to be found of it.

Astronomy "came into being" — though during about two millennia historical documents show of no progress worth mentioning.

Weidner points to a text from Nippur as one of the first astronomical evidences, about the time of passing from the third to the second millenium b.C. — It gives two measurings of distances between fixed stars so remarkably accurate, that astronomy in Babylonia must have been standing at an almost unbelievable height at that time. Moreover, this text shows that babylonian astronomers then already made use of a system of coördinates, measuring from the aequator, to determine places of stars in the firmament. — Babylonian astronomy thus had reached a height which excites our amazement at the time of the first dynasty of Babylon and that of the Sealand.

In the 18th century b.C. the people of the Kassites descended from the mountains of Zagros and ruled for about 500 years over Babylon, during which time culture and science did not make much progress.

As to documents we possess from this period an astrological text of Nippur and

[1]) On the deification of kings Kugler has an entire chapter in his IInd book (SSB, 1909, p. 144).

on the other side the star-lists and astrological texts of Boghaz-Köi. As the astronomical professional expressions in these texts are perfect, scientific astronomy can only have been progressing slowly afterwards. Later, when the rulership of the Kassites had been broken and Babylonians again seized the hands of Marduk, a new era of great flourishing sets in. From the time of Ashurbanipal then dates the next purely astronomical text with measurings of the positions of fixed stars and again with the use of the aequatorial coördinates system. Then follows the first ephemeris, from the 37th year of Nebukadnezar; it has extremely accurate astronomical observations. From then onward we possess astronomical texts in uninterrupted order of succession up to the beginning of our era.

As regards babylonian astrology the library of Ashurbanipal contains texts of this sort which must have been compiled about 4500 b. C. or at least antidated to that time; from the time of Sargon of Agade (about 2850 b. C.) date the oldest astrological omina in history, which are contained in the great work on omina *Enuma Anu (il) Enlil.* Others follow from the time of Tiriḳḳan, king of Gutium, of Ibi-Sin, king of Ur, and so forth, until the time of Nebukadnezar I, the king of the dynasty of Pashe [1]). As to originals from the time before the Sargonides the oldest are from the time of the dynasty of the Kassites and were written about 1500. This is the Nippur text mentioned before, which alas is not dated more accurately, and the astrological texts of Boghaz-Köi. Chronologically follow the astrological documents from the time of the Sargonides. Of the later babylonian period we possess only very little publications of originals [2]). Next comes the babylonian legacy to the hellenistic Greeks and Romans, to the Indians, and so on. Earlier already astrological knowledge went over from Babylon to China. This is the development of Babylonian astrology drawn in great lines. Thus Weidner, whose work intended to contain three books, which would deal with the fixed stars (I), the Moon, the Sun and the planets (II) and meteorology (III). Only book I has appeared.

"The mass of material in store enables us to form an almost complete reconstruction."

At first sight it might appear that the definition as 'astrological' was used by the author where only astronomical measurings were done. The reason for these measurings and the additional qualifications regarding the heavenly bodies that were observed, however, gave the full right to the justification of the title 'astrological'.

The astronomical indications as fundamentals of this 'starry mythology' are rather sparsely worked out, however. I have never been able to find anything of the nature of a concrete horoscope. The conviction exists, however, that the constellations ruling at the birth of a child were observed and were esteemed to find their analogy in that birth. This is not a worked out horoscope and the etymology of the word points to hellenistic times, in which the development of exact science together with a general philosophic mentality of the Greeks take the lead. We find a text, in which is said that "when Ishtar (Venus) rises in the East at the birth of a child, it (or its life) promises to be peaceful and wealthy, and where it goes, there it will be loved, all its days long". There are more suchlike; so in particular the text given by F. Thureau-Dangin from the Louvre (AO. 6483), which dates from the period of the Seleucides. But in general the conviction rules, which was so remarkably well defined by Jeremias. that the original astromical foundations for this vision of life had to be regarded of old more as a book of images, only later becoming a ciphering-book. (HAOG, p. 202 and 244, 356, also in the introduction to the 2nd ed.).

An important work to the knowledge of the astronomical grounds is that by Ch. Virolleaud in 14 parts, of which 7 in cuneiform characters and 7 transcribed, containing about 350 texts, divided into 4 books under the titles Shamash, Sin, Ishtar, Adad respectively.

We further find a good deal of material given by Alfred Jeremias, Carl Bezold, Bruno Meissner, Morris Jastrow, F. X. Kugler and others.

---

[1]) = Isin II.

[2]) In the mean time important new publications have been made, chiefly by F. Thureau-Dangin from texts of Uruk.

The exact calculating of the places of planets, Sun and Moon in a horoscopic scheme seems to have made its appearance only later on in the hellenistic period. A very interesting Demotic text, published by Erman and Krebs has been found in Egypt dating from the 25th year of the reign of the Emperor Augustus (which means 6 b.C.) relating the position of the planets in the zodiac (or the constellations?). Babylonian-assyrian culture then belongs to the past.

Birth-omina, of which a great many are known to have been found in the library of Ashurbanipal (668—626 b.C.), as well as many texts related by Virolleaud, but also other omina-texts *e.g.* from Boghaz-Köi, are for the greater part not of a direct astrological nature, but take significance from either meteorological facts or monstruous birth-phenomena; very seldom star-influences are named. Another wide spread practice in the every-day life of the Babylonians and much favoured by popular interest was the predicting from the liver of a sacrified animal. Predictions appear to have been done mostly in this way and, as far as we may judge from the present literature at hand, more rarely from meteorological phenomena, and only exeptionally from eclipses and other heavenly constellations. Progressive or predictive horoscopes are wanting as well as birth-horoscopes.

III. MONOTHEISM?

As so many omina, relating to predictions concerning persons and general happenings, belong to a niveau much lower and of a much lesser cosmic influence than those of Sun, Moon and planets, the fact is evident, that we have to acknowledge that the greater part of every-day-life under the babylonian civilisation, was not so much specifically astrological as is thought sometimes. Perhaps we must rather say that the average man in daily life realised only a relatively low sediment of the said culture and that its descent was hardly to be recognised therein.

Cannot the same fact be stated in every great civilisation? There are a good many layers or levels of development in every humanity. A very clear conception was given by Baentsch in his work on monotheism in Mesopotamia. In his introduction he says:

Certainly the whole of the ancient Orient represents a grand, all-embracing, imposing unity of culture, and Israel belongs so much to this unity, as an organic part of it and within it, that the history of this people is not to be understood without granting its relation with this culture (AIM, p. VI).

Albeit that we may accept with much probability that the Jews show a remarkable and preceeding analogy with the Calvinists, in so far as in te midst of their surroundings in the near East they accentuated the supreme One-God-idea and apparently (gradually?) dropped the images of the other gods in their manifoldedness, this exposing of the extrinsic god has not at all given a solution of a very remarkable nature, because: plurality culminates anyhow in unity.

Baentsch continues: At first sight it appears as foolishness, trying to find in the ancient Orient anything that resembles monoteism. Everywhere we encounter, wherever we look, clearly and extensively worked out, polytheism. This relates to Babylon and Assyria as well as to Arabia and Egypt, to Syria as well as to Phoenica and Kanaän. Wherever we look gods innumerable (AIM, p. VI).

The recent researches by Prof. Frankfort on the Tell-Asmar, East of the Tigris, in the winter of 1933/1934, made him utter the supposition that perhaps these different images of gods, among the Sumerians at least, are properly speaking only aspects of one God, *i.e.* the god of fertility.

Delitzsch suggested — as Baentsch quotes — that along the way of etymology an explanation may be given for the word *el*, the word for 'god', bearing a strongly monotheistic tendency — be it more or less problematic — and at least for a certain group of the ancient Semites, the Western Semites or Amorites.

Essentially Baentsch points out a difference between three threads, as it were knotted into one chord, *i.e.* that of the national religion of the people, that of the devoted of heart and soul, finally that of the priests religion. Asking whether traces of monotheism are to be found in the latter, the answer must be in the negative as regards the religion of the people. Another question is that about the national religion in the higher sense, because such a pantheon has always its monarchistic culmination-point — and this is a fact to which we indeed must pay attention (AIM, p. 6).

In this way Marduk is the *summus deus* of Babylon, especially since the time of Hammurabi.

One must consider that these local gods and popular gods in the essence ot their nature were more than local numina. Partially they had their cosmic significances, as *e.g.* the greater divine tri-unity *Anu*, *Enlil*, *Ea*, partly; and for the greater part indeed they were astral gods, heavenly gods, whose manifestations were seen in the planets (AIM, p. 7).

Exactly as in Babylonia we find matters in Assyria. — The local god Assur counts as the king of the gods, having built the heaven of Anu and the underworld of the earth, and throned in the splendid heaven, etc... (AIM, p. 10).

A propos of monotheism, may we not remember *Genesis* I, where God, the One, is said to have created Heaven and Earth? — *Genesis* being derived from the same source of culture, of which Baentsch and Böhl are speaking, comparison lies near at hand.

Of the Hymns Baentsch says ...all is in all: the lecture of the divine hymns gives more than once the lively sensation, as if a higher and purer knowledge of God comes to be expressed... which certainly relates to the second category, the religion of the devote. The same is strongly represented in the presently known documents, penitential psalms, in invocations, dedications and consecrations.

After Kirchner's *Wörterbuch der philosophischen Grundbegriffe* henotheism — this is what Baentsch hints at — means — Max Müller is quoted — "a preceeding stadium of monotheism, in which indeed one popular god is honoured, but the existence of other gods is not denied."

In Babylonian theology the divine personalities are generally represented as the god 'and his wife', in which the latter plays no separate rôle, however, but the divine principle appears to be used in every instance in which a femine expression takes place; Alfred Jeremias says: in this way the relatively highest divine image does not reach higher than duality — not yet unity.

It is worth the trouble to quote literally what Baentsch says of the priests religion, because we shall have to consider it as the source of knowledge of everything that could be innerly known and understood. Not what the people believed, but what the priests knew, is important.

"...Next to their duties of public worship the priests colleges were obliged to learn the description of the gods nature and their functions in the heavens, to understand scientifically the results in a theological doctrine. These priestly doctrinal systems have come indeed to a remarkable monotheism. To understand this monotheism one has to bear always in mind, that the ancient babylonian religion (dating back from the Sumerians), is a starreligion after its nature. In the stars it sees the divine powers working and ruling; the planets to them are the transmitters of the orders, the interpreters of the divine will. In this way the acknowledgement of the gods could only be reached by the way of astronomical studies. Consequently theological science with the ancient Babylonians was fundamentally astrology." (AIM, p. 20).

We shall want all our attention for these expressions: the piece of paper on which a royal decree has been printed, communicating the royal will and intention, is as little the king himself, as a physical planet could ever be esteemed to be the godhead himself, though actually they demonstrate certain phenomena as a particular way of expression, relating to It, which in itself again may be as a particular aspect of the Supreme, the Almighty, the One. — How could it well be otherwise?

Undoubtedly one thing stands firm with all these researchers, being the essential in the vision of life of the learned Babylonians: "To the ancient Babylonians existed as an axiom, the image of the world accurately resembles that of the heavens" (AIM, p. 21).

Consequently: 'as above – so below '– as the saying of old ran. (Compare HAOG, p. 139).

They make a difference between the earthy and the heavenly universe, of which the first is only the mirrored reflection of the latter (AIM, p. 21).

If we accept this idea, we will have to grant the supposition, however, that the image of heaven has to be considered as more abstract, more spiritual, than the earthy image. And if this be the case, this conception of the Babylonians is not far from analogous with that of the present Christian thought on Divinity, after which the abstract Lord and Almighty, the God as Christians think Him, is called the creator of this world at the same time.

IV. THE COSMICAL TRIAD

As the earthy universe was divided into three parts, the aerial heaven, the domain of the earth and the ocean which encircled the earth as well as existed under the earth, in the same way the heavenly universe was to be divided into three parts, in the Northern Heaven, in the Zodiacal Belt or the earthy domain in heaven which was considered as a sort of encircling bulwark and upon which the seven planets grinded their way in their courses, and the Southern Heaven, or Heavenly Ocean. Three gods are ruling the heavenly, as well as the earthy universe. Over the Northern Heaven and its parallel the Heaven of Air on earth, the god Anu ruled, over the Zodiacal Belt and its earthy parallel the earthy domain, rules the god Enlil, lord of the 'lands', over the Southern Heaven and its earthy parallel the ocean, Ea rules, god of the deep of the water and of abysmal wisdom. These three gods, Anu, Enlil and Ea, represent the upper triad of gods, the supreme babylonian trinity, which stands on top of all the rest of the divine world. Within this divine triad a monarchistic culmination takes place. Their *summus deus* is Anu, the king of the gods. To him belongs the Northern Heaven and he has his throne in the summit of the universe, the northern point or North-Pole of the heavens, which as the throne of the highest god naturally possessed the character of the highest sanctity. This explains the remarkable sanctity of the north of which we find clear evidences in the Old Testament (AIM, p. 21).

Anu is the god in short finally; he is called also *ilu*...; the praefix *il* comes in use as a general expression for the idea of a god.

The library of King Ashurbanipal — and another specimen derived from the collection of Boghaz-Köi — shewed that the Babylonians in their drawing of the heavens for the determination of the places of stars and planets divided them into three parts, which were called after and analogous with the great participation in three of the universe: under Anu, Enlil (Bēl) and Ea. They must have been dating from about 4000 b.C (Weidner HBA, p. 66/75).

In an essay on *Der Altbabylonische Götterkreis* (SSB, Book II, 1909) Kugler has: As the highest divinity ruling life on earth counted, from the remotest historical times down to the dynasty of Larsa, *En-lil (Bēl)*. The oldest texts have the orthography *(En-lil)*, which means the ruler of the region of air. This is confirmed by the fact, that the storm is his weapon and the Moon drifting through the air is his son.

Next to *En-lil* we find two other great cosmic gods, already early in history, under Gudea, who together with *En-lil* constitute the one all-embracing triad: *Anu*, god of the heaven of the fixed stars, and *En-ki*, the god of the (earthy) deep. (SSB, p. 133/134).

Anu is called 'the highest in power' — 'the lord of countries'.

That which was mentioned by Baentsch induces Böhl to the remark, that never yet a real monotheism is reached, because this expression can only mean the extrinsic or transcendental god, while with the Babylonians the divine world is always immanent; included within their earthy world.

With regard to this we come to the great problem of transcendancy and immanence. The latter indeed means 'being in the world'. It does not mean a concrete visible and palpable existence, however; and this probably is difficult to realise for a good many people. There is much that doesn't exist in this world *in concreto*. The gods — as such — are abstract but Plato called them the motives (motoric forces), *theoi,* who not only take part in the world, but are propelling it and consequently constitute the contents of it. The greatest godhead, the Almighty, can only be an abstraction and the highest abstraction and highest motive, the motoric force urging to the highest. This confirms the conception of the Calvinist and the Jew about this extrinsic god. But is this actually extrinsic? Where Jew and Calvinist while living in this world speak of Him and are full of Him — how can He be outside them? Apparently the extrinsic idea of god — or the extrinsic god as an idea — under the influence of modern astronomy, physics with its electron and relativity theories, finally modern astrology, will be proved undoubtedly to be an abstraction and to return immediately to immanence.

Much as the last decennia have gathered in the knowledge of assyrian history and babylonian civilisation, we have not seen any broader standpoint as yet than that which speaks in Dupuis' Introduction to his *Origine de tous les Cultes* of the end of the 18th century, where he calls: ... The descent of the gods, children of the two primæval causes, of heaven and earth... — which two primæval causes are further elucidated in this line: "from the divergence of causes I come to that of the principles, which are divided in a principle of light and good, and a principle of darkness and evil; which embraces the foundations of all religions." Dupuis is speaking openly of principles and regards the gods as descending from the same. Consequently... as principles or abstractions as well.

What renders the interpretation of historical documents on this matter so difficult, is the contents of these documents. They treat of the mystery of creation, of the problem of life and death and everything between. Rightly Alfred Jeremias says that to be able to decipher the same *one must understand the language of the mystery.* Perhaps this language is no longer understood by the greater part of the learned researchers of archaeology and theology in this time of a crisis in the regions of the vision of life which appears to be more dangerous even than that in economics. The word 'mystery' has got a suspect sound to western ears, even if the West may have come over the point where it proclaimed: there is no mystery.

In the meantime we are compelled to admiration with regard to the multitude of documents in clay, accounts, letters, annals, collected during the last half of a century. Much is treated on astronomy and astrology.

One of the principal theses of the babylonian vision of life and world is that of the general periodicity in everything. Justly says Boll therefore: In determined periods the stars return to their courses and once — after a long long time — they will all be together again on the point from which they started. Thus every happening on earth will have to repeat itself in the new era as it was in the old one. (*Sternglaube und Sterndeutung* p. 97). We may leave alone that the period mentioned after which everyone of the planets will be back again on the point of an earlier period, must be indicated by a cipher so great that every human imagination is baffled by it — the fundamental idea of cyclic happening in itself is important and is proved from a good many documents to have been a fundamental idea of all babylonian culture. Directive thinking is in general that of the West, thinking in circular courses is of the East... says Jeremias. (HAOG p. 26).

The greatest cycle in the heavens, that could speak to human observation, will probably have been that of the precession of the equinoxes. There once was an important difference of opinion between Assyriologists about the question whether the precession was actually known to the ancient Mesopotamians. Some pretend — amongst them Father F. X. Kugler S. J. — that it was Hipparchus of Nikea, the Greek, who discovered the precessional movement of the equinoxes; other researchers, however, take it — immediate proofs are wanting — that long ago babylonian culture knew the precession and that one of the indications about this fact — I again abstain from the word *proof* — would be the pretention that the later periods ascribed the whole of their knowledge to a 'period of the Twins', when our earthy vernal equinox stood in the constellation of the Twins. This zodiacal 'sign', the Twins, possesses the faculty, as every astrologer now knows, to connect, to unite (c. q. heaven and earth, consequently), to communicate knowledge from the heavens to the people of the earth — and this was considered to be the case from old times and as far as astrologers existed.

Meissner judges that Kidinnu already knew the difference between the tropical and the siderial year, which means the difference of the precession. May be that we will have to accept that Hipparchus took over this element and the doctrine of the precession from his babylonian colleagues without mentioning their names together with their calculations of the phases of the Moon and indications about Jupiter. (BA, II, p. 418). Bringing back the matter to Kidinnu, who was one of the heads of the astronomers' school at Sippar, shortly after the death of Alexander the Great (about 323 b.C.), would not make such an important difference, because Hipparchus lived about 150 b.C. It only would mean that the invention was not Hipparchus' and derived from babylonian source.

In his last book (1924) of the series *Sternkunde und Sterndienst* Kugler comes again on the question of the discovery of the precession and denies even that Kidinnu has found it out. It doesn't matter much for our astrological conceptions, if we have to thank either Hipparchus or Kidinnu for it.

In the same work *Sternkunde und Sterndienst in Babel* Father Kugler repeatedly protests against the too far reaching expectations of Hugo Winckler and Pan-Babylonists in general, with regard to early astronomical knowledge in Mesopotamia. So we read in his IInd book, Part II (1909, p. 25) how even a phenomenon as the total eclipse of the Sun, which only happens in so total a way about once in a hundred years, and is so clearly observable, was, in the year 763 b.C., only indicated by the simple communication: "in the month Sivan an eclipse of the Sun took place" — which, says Kugler, hardly can be accounted for as an astronomical observation. "Other 'astronomical" indications of the older time assyro-babylonian star-gazers show similarly a want of interest in measurings of space and time on the starry heavens".

An elaborate astronomical observation would not be in its place in a list of eponym officials, says Böhl in answer to Kugler.

With regard to lack of accuracy in observations of the planets Kugler gives several specimina (SSB, p. 20/21).

Another point is this, that longitude and latitude as astronomical coördinates do not make their appearance before the second century b.C., says Kugler.

He devotes a special chapter in his IInd book to the question of the precession and strongly contradicts the standpoint of Weidner and others, taking for granted that the Babylonians must have known the Twin-, the Bull- and the Ram-period of the precession. Kugler says: nothing proves it, but the lack of accurate calculation and observation leaves no doubt as to the absence of scientific astronomy proper (SSB, p. 24 etc.). "... The perfectly unscientific calculation of time in those days (*i. e.* those of Sargon the Akkadian.-Th.) and even in the next 2000 years, is inconsistent with the care of the systematic observation of the heavens, without which it would be impossible to discover a change so difficult to detect as that. Consequently we cannot speak of any knowledge of the ancient Babylonians about the precession" (SSB, p. 30). A positive dictum follows: "The Babylonians were ignorant of the precession at least until the middle of the second century (b.C.) (SSB, p. 31).

Böhl says that Kugler goes too far with his denial towards the Babylonians in this matter. Perhaps not everybody on the other hand will accept the very decisive conviction of Alfred Jeremias' writing: .... The question if the Sumerians have already observed and known the simple fact of the displacement of the vernal equinox, I must answer in the affirmitive now as before. Nay against everyone of the lively contentions one has to retort the question: how were it possible that they should not have known the fact? Kugler by combating it intended 'to throw down the pillars of Pan-Babylonism' and to deliver the world from the 'curse of Babel'. Astronomers who have mixed in the discussion, rightly pointed to the fact that Aristoteles, who did not precisely exaggerate foreign science, still addicted to the Babylonians a continued observation of the heavens during many hundreds of years and that such a continual observation of the heavens could not have disregarded the precession of the equinoxes in the course of time. The fixing of the commencement of the year in a certain point of the Sun's orbit, is an indirect proof of it. It presupposes the measuring of the Suns' place and the Sun's orbit. This cannot only have been computed with the heaven's equator. (HAOG, p. 239, 240).

Says Jeremias: the simple statement of the precessionnal fact without counting the exact calculation of the same must have had considerable results already. It furnished the material of apperception with the creation of the mythos and in particular the cosmic symbolic language to the glorification of the Deliveror, whose work, birth, war with the dragon, martyrdom, death and revival were read from the calendaric phenomena. We must mention, that one of the very important myths — some say poems — treats of the redemption of the world, the theme according to Jeremias being one of the cardinal points of sumerian vision of life. He points to some remarkable phenomena of the cosmic symbolic language, in which the mythos was veiled:

"With the 'Ram' the montly star-symbolism of the Gilgamesh-epos was entered, with the Ram begins the list of montly stars of Boghaz–Köi from the time about 1350. Very cleary we are able to prove the symbolic meaning of that time concerning the vernal position of the Sun (since about Hammurabi) lying within the reach of this constellation, which at least since hellenistic times up to our days was considered as Ram. In older times the constellation, including part of the Cetus, was seen as heavenly arable land upon which the heavenly peasant is ploughing" [1]). Further "... Consequently we can speak of a 'Ram-period' undoubtedly... The conception appears to derive from Egypt, because there the symbolising of the Saviour or His Prophet (which to the oriental mind comes to the same) by the Ram (hellenistic: Arnion) appears to have existed since about the second millennium b.C., like prophetic texts shew. Alexander the Great, who during his life had himself adorned with the splendid coat of cosmic saviour-symbolism, showed it, to give notice of the fact, by putting on the Ram's horns in the oasis of Jupiter-Ammon [2]). In the Revelation of St. John the coming Christ is called the cosmic Ram with ten eyes and ten horns, who after the struggle and the conquest opens the book of fate and enters into worlddominion." (HAOG, p. 240).

When the mighty symbolism of the Revelation of St. John came into being, the Spring-position of the Sun had already entered the sign of the Fishes. So we should expect the initiation into a Fishes-period. Jeremias repeatedly asked the question, if the secret sign of the 'fish' of Christianity, which was later on applied to the name and title of Christ, had to be considered as an intimation to the above mentioned fact. The creative power of the mythos had then already been extinguished for a long time, however, and on the other hand ciphering astronomy did not mind symbolic values. Now we can raise the question if the simple observation of the precessional position in the times before Hammurabi already, *i. e.* in the time when for instance the vernal equinox was standing in the Bull, found symbolic expression. May be the veneration of a white bull next to the symbolically evident worship of the Ram-constellation on another day of the festival, was indication of it at the (Babylonian) New-Year's feast. It might have been an archaic remembrance from the time when the deity-deliverer revealed himself in the Bull. Remarkable as well is the astral symbolism of the 'heavenly bull' sent by the god of the heavens in the battle against Gilgamesh, knightly epic from the time of Hammurabi, which worked on old materials.

A Twin-period appears to have been indicated by the legends, that speak of the founders of dynasties, which begin with the tale of the Dioscuri. Of course this can be explained from archaic fiction. In this way the genialogy was dated back into eternity.

Jeremias again points out, that in the time when the Twins contained the vernal equinox, *i. e.* during the rise of the Sumerians, remarkable figurations were to

---

[1]) Probably the meaning is here that in older times one saw the vernal equinox in the constellation of 'the heavenly field'. Th.

[2]) Oasis of Siwa. Th.

be seen in the heavens, *e.g.* in the first place this that the Milky Way at the moment of the vernal equinox at sunrise stood vertical over the observer, and the same at the autumnal equinox, when the Sun entered into the Archer. (HAOG p. 240—242).

I take the conclusion from this chapter of Jeremias, mentioning that the periods are dated respectively:

the Twins about	6200—4400
the Bull ,,	4400—2000
the Ram ,,	2200— 100
the Fishes ,,	100 b.C.—2000 A.D.

Apparently the data are more or less inaccurate. If we calculate it exactly and start from a fixed point, *i.e.* the conjunction of the vernal equinox with the first point of the constellation Aries, as it after the old persian and other heavenly charts has been indicated on the atlasses of Argelander and Bonn — and others as well — which would make the Ram-period end 100 b.C. (may be 105—108), this period must have begun 2156 years earlier, *i.e.* 2260, the Bull-period 4420, the Twins-period 6580 b.C., leaving apart the difference of 5 or 8 years at the beginning of the precessional zero-point. Kugler gives (IBB p. 149):

Twins:	6534—4383
Bull:	4383—2232
Ram:	2232—81 b.C.,

thus taking 2151 years for one twelfth part of the cycle.

Next to the astronomical arguments may still be called as a witness for this starting-point a remarkable document, the so called *Acta Archelai*, containing a dispute between the bishop Archelaus of Mesopotamia and his opponent Mani, who was considered to be the paraklet by his confessors. Mani's ennemy says: if he really were the paraklet or consoler of whom Christ told that he would come after Him (St. John XIV, 16), he would certainly have come immediately after Jesus, and not, like Mani, more than 300 years later (... *trecentos et eo amplius annos*). Mani lived 214—292 A.D. Deducting 'threehunderd and some' years from Mani's birth, we arrive at about 100 b.C. and taking literally what was said, this must have been the year of Jesus' depart. It is the departure, in the setting of the Golgotha-drama — and not the birth of Christ — which must (symbollically or really) coïncide with the 'offering of the Lamb', the end of the Lamb- or Ram-period. And if 100 b.C. is the end, birth must have taken place about 133 b.C.

The evidence of the *Acta* appears to confirm nicely the astronomical indication.

V. THE MADONNA — WORLD-CREATION

Supreme the idea of the madonna stands in the ancient sumerian cosmical conception; it has transpired into the whole of babylonian culture. Sprung from the religious sagas and epic tales this appears to represent the line of devotion and romantism, imagination and dramatism in this civilisation.

From the triad of the gods Anu, Ea, Enlil, the grand spiritual personifications of the primordial powers creating the universe, keeping it in action and dissolving it, the divine world *in toto* came forth and this is of which theology speaks. And as well the doctrine of gods or motives or motoric forces, that propel and rule the world and keep her running.

Mesopotamia had its *Epic of Creation*, treating of the origin of the gods and their taking to the work of creation. Of the different versions we know nowadays, let here be named those by King, Ungnad, Langdon, Ebeling, Landsberger, Furlani and Deimel. Berosus tells us: "When the universe was still wet and living creatures in it had come to existence, ... it is said, that Bēl, whom we translate as Zeus, has cut the waters into two, separated heaven and earth from eachother and ordained the world. The living creatures, however, not being able to support the power of light, would have perished. Bēl, seeing the land desolate and unfruitful, is said to have ordered to a god, that he should cut him off the head, fructify the earth by mixing it with the outflowing blood and in that way create men and animals, that should be able to support the air. Bēl is said to have created the Sun, the Moon and the five planets" (Meissner, BA, II, p. 103—104).

This legend of creation — says Meissner — was corroborated by the Epic of Creation, which was produced at Babel every year at the New-Year's Festival. (Compare Jeremias, HAOG 117—118).

A close relation between this epic and the first chapter of the biblical book *Genesis* can hardly be passed unnoticed. Is, however this God, who after *Genesis* created heaven and earth, in perfect analogy with Bēl (Marduk), in the Babylonian *Epic of Creation,* then we shall be obliged to see this Bēl or Marduk acting as God and Creator like the God of *Genesis.* With the same sort of reserve, as Blavatsky's *Secret Doctrine* has it: it is not the Supreme Deity (the potential one) who creates worlds, but the Demiurgos, the third aspect (reality). The latter indeed is the function of Zeus in the greek pantheon, as the head of king of the gods, creating, building and motoring the world of experience *i. e.* reality.

Anu on the contrary could be compared with the 'father in heaven', whom the Gospels of the *New Testament* speak of. The analogy may be illustrated with several examples, *e. g.* Ishtar in the *Gilgamesh Epic* brings her complaints before her 'father' Anu, who is in heaven. With Gudea he is 'the Father' and the king of the gods — the literal meaning of Anu is 'heaven' (HAOG p. 348).

The assyrian version of the *Epic of Creation* has that Ashur, the assyrian supreme god, — who often shows very martial features, but who certainly resembles very much the babylonian Marduk, whose place he takes in this *Epic,* — had to combat Tiâmat and her dragons of the chaos. Tiâmat is the feminine entity; it is difficult to say: deity. The proper nature of Tiâmat, as opposed to the nature of Ashur-Marduk-Zeus, Creator or Demiurgos, reminds of course the figure of Satan, but is of a broader importance. Marduk by his successful battle against Tiâmat, is elevated to the rank of 'great god' and head of the lower gods. It is easy to conclude from astrological philosophy as we know it nowadays, that Jupiter-Zeus-Marduk-Ashur, lord of the zodiacal sign Sagittarius, as the master of logical — consequently creative — thinking, conquers Tiâmat or chaos, indicated by the zodiacal sign Cancer, the polar opposite of Capricorn (zodiacal sign of order and the ordained cosmos). In the *Enuma Elish* or *Song of World-Creation* in Babylon, 'Mummu Tiâmat' is called the Mother of (it) All. Compare the *Stanzas of Dzyan* from Blavatsky's *Secret Doctrine* (I), where chaos indeed has the same great cosmic significance as in the *Enuma Elish.* In the same work we find Merodach (Marduk) as the creator *versus* Tiâmat as primordial chaos. Together they are the first androgyne being or duality in cosmos. (SD I, 304 and Section on Chaos-Theos-Cosmos, I, 365. Also 56, 401, 477, 528 ed. 1893).

Langdon says: The Epic was undoubtedly written in the period of the First Babylonian Dynasty, 2225—1926. (After a later and more probable calculation 2057—1757.—Böhl). Although no tablets of the poem have been found on that time it is clear that it comes down from the Sumerians and is pre-babylonic. When battling against Tiâmat, Ashur was armed with the cyclone, preceeded and followed by various gods of the pantheon. The names of Tiâmat's monsters are not given here. (BEC, p. 11) — ... an earlier sumerian poem of a similar kind existed, which inspired the semitic poem, a problem which remains to be examined. The Epic originally contained six books. The hymn to the names of Marduk, which now forms book VII, must have existed as an indepedant poem ... etc. In another version it is Marduk, who conquers Tiâmat and we hear that he (Marduk) is the son of Ea (Neptune). Kingu is exalted over the powers of Chaos and receives the tablets of fate. (BEC, p. 13). Kingu evidently is the personification of chaos. After the conquest by Marduk, Kingu is brought before Ea and destroyed: of his blood mankind was created to honour and to worship the gods. (BEC, p. 15). — Theosophy teaches: Thus mankind was created from the fluidal sphere, which itself is part of the great cosmic ocean, but this can only take place after the conquest of logic or creative Thought *(mahat)* over chaos. (Compare SD).

At any rate the *Epic of Creation* is also a solar mythe and intimately connected with the Spring-Sun, whose return from the region of darkness was celebrated by a long festival at the beginning of the year. (BEC, p. 20).

Marduk is standing as a representative of the highest god, Anu.

Tiâmat has further been called in this poem Ummu Hubur, the Mother Hubur, who 'forms everything'; is also called the 'radiant Tiâmat'. It is the 'great mother', 'mother of the gods' and 'queen of the heavens' in the sense of chaotic reversal of the cycle, *i.e.* in the sense of the underworld. Her counterpart is the upperworld. It is she, in the first lines, who brings forth heaven and earth in the sense of the ancient Aeon. Opposed to Tiâmat and as her original opposite a figure appears which bears a higher name than Marduk or Ashur, *i.e.* Apsû, 'abyss', separated from her and seen as the generator of heaven and earth. This is the intrinsic duality of the world to be created: the lower aspect being that of Marduk and Tiâmat as the unformed materia in the physical world. (HAOG, p. 117—118).

According to Berosus — his communications were confirmed by the cuneiform documents — ten 'pre-fathers' originally ruled over the country, their reigns reaching to an enormous height, the numbers of their years ranging between 10800 years and 64800 years, together forming a total of 432.000 years, during which time they made their people happy. (Ungnad).

This reminds us of the legendary rulers of Egypt of pre-historic dynasties and reminds us as well of the ten *Avatâras* of Indian theosophy, whom Blavatsky in her *Secret Doctrine*, part I, calls "special incarnations of the World-Spirit in Man" (p. 83, foot-note) and also "manifestations unto man" (p. 730); in the IInd Part "divine incarnations of the Universal Spirit" (p. 502); in Part III a whole chapter is devoted to Cycli and Avatâras, in which the author says that the number 432 is full of cosmic significance in evolution and that "these figures were adopted by all the older nations, such as those of Egypt and Chaldaea, etc., ..." (p. 345).

Evidently 4320 is the sixth part of the Sidereal Year or cycle of the precession: 25920 years (this number is very often mentioned instead of 25868). According to Mrs. Blavatsky there are cycles within greater cycles, which are all contained in the one Kalpa of 4.320.000 years. (S D III p. 346).

VI. THE HEAVENLY OR CYCLICAL TRIAD

THE SEVEN PLANETS

The cosmic triad of gods was repeated in a heavenly triad specially charged with earthy affairs. Generally the order of succession if given as Sin, Shamash, Ishtar (the latter sometimes replaced by Adad). Sin is the Moon, Shamash the Sun, Ishtar 'the star', more particular meaning the planet Venus. Adad is the name for the god of the stormy weather. One could call him perhaps: king of the atmosphere. In its design of beginnings the Epic of Creation with its doctrine of tri-unity, clearly demonstrates the foundations upon which all the rest of theogony will be constructed: on those of heaven, earth and underworld. This is also the foundation of the symbolic map of the world, which was drawn with Babylon in the centre: the earth as a plain, being itself the separation between an upper- and a lower-halfglobe, the upper or northern representing that of the heavens, the lower or southern that of the underworld. The babylonian and sumerian siqqurats, towers built in subsequent stages, and the assyrian ones which are designed in spirally winding ascents, perhaps point to the wish to reach as high as possible into the heavens and to express the gradations of heavenly conditions.

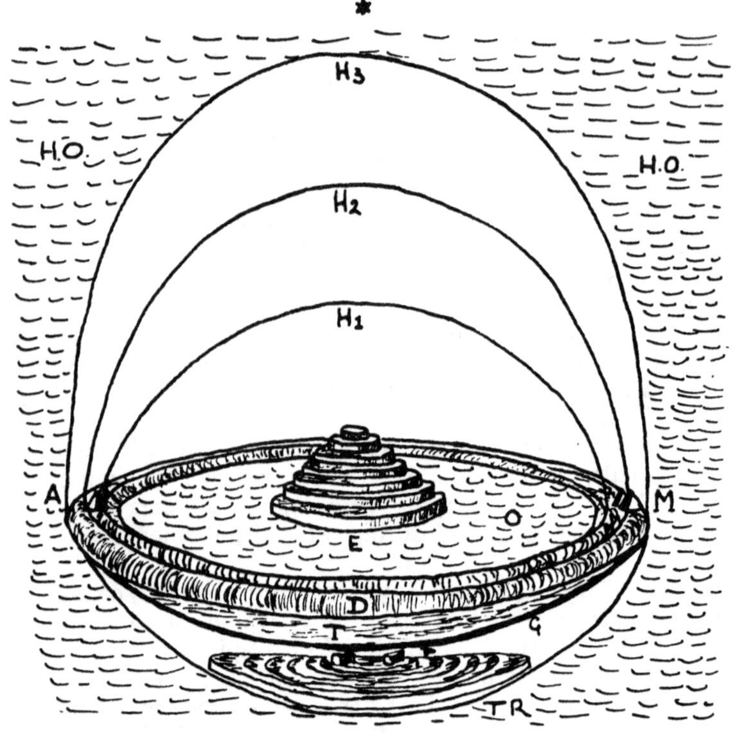

The babylonian image of the world. (taken from Boll, Sternglaube und Sterndeutung)

E	the earth;
$H_1H_2H_3$	the first, second, third heaven;
HO	heavenly ocean;
O	earthy ocean;
T, G,	de depth and bottom of the earthy ocean;
A	the evening (West), the two mountains of sunset;
M	the morning (East), the two mountains of sunrise;
D	the heavenly dam;
TR	the seven walls and the palace (P) of the kingdom of death.

We modern astrologers shall easily see that in all astrological interpretation in the first place we must take notice of the three great cosmic domains or kingdoms: heaven, earth and underworld.

In their turn Sin, Shamash, Ishtar are analogous with the ruling principles of heaven (Shamash, the Sun), earth (Ishtar, Venus) and the waters of the deep (Sin, the Moon). The birth of Ishtar from the waters according to the babylonian idea may perhaps be compared with the legend of the birth of Aphrodite in Greece afterwards and with the place in *Genesis* I (9), where 'the dry land' appeared from the waters. Shamash is, in many respects, only to be seen as the solar god, the hero, Apollo driving the solar chariot.

This second triad of gods thus very soon enters the regions of reality and undoubtedly the heavenly bodies are indicated as the dwelling places, the carriages or embodiments of the divine principles, *c.q.* beings. Nowhere a similar reference is made as to the abodes of the Upper-triad: Anu, Bēl (Enlil) and Ea are the principles which later, in modern astrology, we shall find back in the outer planets, sometimes called 'mystery-planets', Uranus, Pluto and Neptune. Astronomically these planets were of course not known in Babylon. In how far any planets at all can be judged to be the embodiments or phenomena of principles as abstract and high as that, we shall leave out of the question here. Modern astrology nevertheless has to say something on this theme. True: in the sense of the Gnosis Anu, Enlil, Ea are with regard to the foundation of things also relatively lower divine spirits. (HAOG, p. 326, 348).

Sin, Shamash, Ishtar are called the trinity of cycles (HAOG, p. 355) and therein comes to expression the great difference between the former and the latter trinity, *i.e.* respectively seen as static and as dynamic. Static are the three great kingdoms of heaven, earth and underworld; wonderfully instructive are these three categories, later on better known under the names dating from the hellenistic period: theos, cosmos, chaos. Compare a chapter on these ideas in the first part of Blavatsky's *Secret Doctrine* (1 p. 365). Chaos is the kingdom of the waters, fluids, matter in condition of solution; cosmos, the kingdom of the cristallised or formed world of phenomena, just like chaos could be called in a certain respect the world of noumena, and if so in every sense; theos the power which causes formation to come forth out of the abstract or the condition of solution. The doctrine of cycles is a teaching so general and so dominating in the babylonian world-conception, that we cannot be astonished seeing the idea represented by the circular movements of the heavenly bodies. To the Babylonians these apparent cyclic movements of the heavenly bodies around the Earth are the immediate motoric causes of the world of historical events. This is perhaps less strange than the fact that they do not appear any longer in our times. Because it is perfectly natural; and the only question that puzzles us, is in how far the Babylonians were really conscious of the actual value of these symbols, *i.e.* of the immanence of the divine or 'heavenly' powers in the heavenly bodies. It is certainly possible that during the 3000 years, which our historical survey covers, immanence and transcendancy have also mingled and struggled with eachother in the mesopotamian plain among the different groups and personalities who played the prominent rôles. Why should we try to enforce a uniform conception about these principles from history, if a perfect evidence is wanting?

Certain is, however, that the heavenly bodies were always used as symbols. What man may have imagined behind them and by means of these symbols, we must leave to the consideration of man himself on his subsequent stages of spiritual evolution; it can hardly be expected in a single formula or definition.

If, however, the heavenly bodies demonstrate the cyclical idea, the actual cycle of everyone of them will of course carry the significance of a specimen of the cyclical process *in toto*. The action takes place between the planet and our earth *c.q.* our own human nature. If we say it this way the thesis will probably not encounter much contradiction and we leave totally apart what people may have thought and cherished in the way of interpretation.

We wish to point here to the relief hewn in the rock near Maltaja[1]), addicted to the assyrian king Sanherib and dating from about 700 b.C. On it the seven gods — planetary gods — are represented each standing erect upon an animal, carrying him. In symbolic and mystic language the comparison is well known between man as the thinker or spiritual entity and his physical body as the 'animal', the charger to the fighter: St. Francis of Assisi still knew the simile and proved it by calling, at his death-bed, his body 'his poor brother the ass', whom he had granted too little food and treated too much on the stick.

Jastrow in his *Babylonian and Assyrian Birth-Omens* treating the different methods of divination, says: In the case of astrology the underlying theory rested on the supposed complete correspondence between movements and phenomena in the heavens and occurrences on earth. The gods being identified with the heavenly bodies — with the Moon, Sun, planets and fixed stars — or as we might also put it the heavenly bodies being personified as gods, the movements in the heavens were interpreted as representing the activity of the gods, preparing the events on earth. Therefore he who could read the signs of the heavens aright would know what was to happen here below. Astrology corresponded in a measure to the modern meteorological observatory enabling one to ascertain a little in advance what was certain to happen, sufficiently so in order to be prepared for it. (BABO, p. 3). Indeed we find the influence of the heavenly bodies called 'the scripture of the heavens', meaning the complicated movements of the Sun, Moon and planets (stars) and their significances.

The doctrine of cycles thus contains the idea that a writing takes place in the heavens dictating the happenings on earth: *viz.* cyclically. Then if we take that the relief of Maltaja means to express that the planetary gods appear as soul *and* body — or rather body *and* soul, which certainly emphasizes the spiritual or psychical contents of the heavenly bodies — we must understand that the thesis of correspondence between heaven and earth reaches much farther than a superficial electro-magnetic theory could explain. Taking this deeper meaning for granted, the movements in the heavens and the happenings on earth as well as the actions of man himself, appear

[1]) vide fig. on p. 48.

to bear altogether a symbolical meaning and to be the expressions of the spiritual and psychical contents of life itself. This conclusion may perhaps be the key to problems and lead to definitions of religion. It is in fact all a problem of religious nature and we cannot escape from it. Moreover we come to the definition of 'divine' forces and influences as meaning motoric or psychical (spiritual), in the same way as Plato called the planets gods: divine and immanent-motoric becomes synonimous in this way of thinking. We may — or rather we must — even draw the perfect consequence of the same idea and put that the Most High is the highest immanent-motoric principle in mankind and in the world.

The documents mention seven planets, including Sun and Moon, which are considered as 'planetary' evidently. Jeremias in his HAOG has: the seven planets rule the world — said the Sabians after Dimeshqi. The Sumerians called them LU BAT MESH, 'roaming sheep', contrary to the fixed starry 'sheep'. How old is the collectivity of the seven? There is no period of intuitive contemplation of the heavens conceivable, in which the three great heavenly bodies, Moon, Sun and Venus, together with the other four planets, Mercury, Mars, Jupiter, Saturn, are wanting, moving through the world of the fixed stars along the heavenly road, about 50 degrees of arc wide. Contradictory to this Diodorus (30.3) is quoted, who ascribes to the Babylonians only five 'interpreters', *i.e.* Venus, Mercury, Mars, Jupiter, Saturn, leaving out of account the Moon and the Sun. One forgets however, that he immediately adds (30.7) the Sun and the Moon, just like assyrian lists of planets mention the Sun and the Moon, before the five planets, adding below: 'these are the seven planets'. The author suggests that an explanation could hardly relate to anything but the seven planets including Sun and Moon — regarding these temples with towers of seven terraces ('the seven UB' — or with Gudea 'the seven UR'), the latter meaning the seven 'transmitters' — of the orders? — or of life? — between heaven and earth. That Diodorus counts the Moon and the Sun separately is true. In the case of the symbols on boundary-stones and *stèles* Moon, Sun and Venus.

The planetary lists dating from assyrian times with their old sumerian names, make the five planets follow after the Moon and the Sun, according to astrological considerations:

1. III R. 57, 65—67a (= CT XXVI, 45, 19—21):
^{il}Sin u ^{il}Shamash = Moon and Sun
^{il}SHUL PA È = Jupiter
^{kakkab}DIL BAT = Venus
^{kakkab}LU BAT (kakkab) SAG USH (kaimânu) = Saturn
^{kakkab}LU BAT GÚ UD = Mercury
ul (= ^{kakkab})ZAL BAT-a-nu = Mars.

Subscribed: These are the seven planets (HAOG, p. 173).

In the first part of his *Sternkunde und Sterndienst in Babel* (1907) Father Kugler mentions the same surname for the planets 'roaming sheep', he mentions Diodorus in the same way and he gives us two slightly different tables of 'the seven planets': (from the list II R./48—54)

	Sumerian		Babylonian-Assyrian:	
1.	(*dingir*) A KU	= (*ilu*)	30 = Sin	= Moon
2.	(*dingir*) *Kashshebi*	= (*ilu*)	UTU = Shamash.	= Sun
3.	(*dingir*) *Da-pi-nu*	= (*ilu*)	SHUL PA UD DU A [1]) . . .	= Jupiter
4.	(*dingir*) *Zib*	= (*ilu*)	*Dilbat*	= Venus
5.	(*dingir*) *Lu-lim*	= (*ilu*)	LU BAT SAG USH = Kaimanu .	= Saturn
6.	(*dinger*) *Bi-ib-bu*	= (*ilu*)	LU BAT GUD UD	= Mercury
7.	(*dingir*) SI-mu-tu	= (*ilu*)	ZAL BAT-a-nu	= Mars (SSB, p. 7-9).

Remarkable is the fact of Saturn being indicated as 'the star of the Sun', and Jupiter as 'the shepherd'.

Kugler doesn't absolutely agree on the point of naming the seven collectively: concerning the taking together of the Sun and Moon with the five planets, and the

[1]) Better reading: SHUL PA È A.

calling them LU. BAT (*bibbu*)stars, we must be careful not to draw the conclusion of 'seven planetary gods' in a closed unity (SSB. p. 11).

The differences in the names do mean different adjectives or circumscriptions generally. Kugler mentions 'sublime son', also 'child' and 'radiating (royal) cap' for the Moon; 'the terrible (hell)' and also 'radiating lord' for Jupiter; 'evening star' and also 'heraldess of the day' for Venus; The 'constant' for Saturn; the 'strong or valiant one' for Mercury (SSB p. 9—10).

A remakable denomination further is that of AN or *Anu* for Mars, (SSB p. 12) which, however, is not astonishing to astrologers, because in a certain way Mars is to be considered as the ruler of the first zodiacal sign, Aries, consequently as lord of the first kingdom. In this way the Assyrians may have viewed their martial god Ashur: when so taken Ashur and Anu may be considered as synonymous.

The planets — described in different ways by their surnames — are the gods in effigy: *Sin, Shamash, Marduk, Ishtar, Nergal, Nebo, Ninurta.*

The seven are taken as three and four. Three — Sin, Shamash, Ishtar — evidently appear to be the reflection or phenomena of the upper triad. The four, Marduk, Nergal, Nebo, Ninurta, are particularly to be identified with the four cardinal points of *the* cycle — *i.e.* evidently every cycle. The latter are perhaps best known in the course of the Sun through the seasons and of the Moon through her phases.

The four planets, as the rulers of the Moon's phases, are bearing the names indicating the principles of the same; in the solar year they bear the names of the four seasons.

In the moral and spiritual sense — modern astrology teaches — these four planets must be taken as representatives of:

— *birth* (midwinter-point), the phase of Saturn-Nergal, which means the germ, seed or concentration;

— *growth* (vernal-equinox), which is the phase of Jupiter-Marduk, and means emanation, elevation, extension, expansion, etc.;

— *decline* after reaching the culmination point of growth, *i.e.* the beginning of dying (mid-summer-solstitium), indicated by the death of the solar child, the phase of Mars-Ninurta, which means the principle of consumption, consuming that which has been grown;

— *conversion* finally of all that was orientated outwardly into inner consciousness (autumnal equinox), the phase of Mercury-Nebo, ruling the transition from the consciousness of awakeness to that of dreaming, exoteric into esoteric being and the turning of the profane into the condition of initiation.

In concordance with the four great cardinal points of the year, the four planets appear very much the same as the four Maharajahs in Hindu mythology, rulers of the four winds of which Saturn rules the South, where the Sun stands in Mid-Winter, Jupiter the East and Spring, Mars the North and Mid-Summer, Mercury the West and Autumn. As such the four planets again show four phases of one whole. Baentsch says: The four planetary gods thus are intrinsically not independent gods, but only '*Teil-Erscheinungen*' (separate appearances) of the One Great God, who works through the Sun (AIM, p. 29).

'Working through' — the One Great God consequently is seen by Baentsch not as the Sun, but as working through the Sun, wich apparently is its physical appearance, vehicle or body.

'*Teil-Erscheinungen*' is the word he uses —'*Teilwesen*' calls Dr. L. Staudenmaier in his book *Die Magie als Experimentelle Naturwissenschaft* the separate entities of consciousness in the totality of a human being.

In another place Baentsch draws the comparison with Egypt. There as well, says he, we see precisely the same speculative ideas, the same monotheism inspiring consideration as in ancient Babylon. The Egyptian religion was also essentially a star-religion and the god who played the principal rôle in it, was the solar god (AIM, p. 35). The other gods were considered as partial conditions, phenomena of this god (AIM, p. 36).

Actually the planets are of course parts of the astronomical organic system, which is the solar system and not independent entities in themselves.

In another place we find Mercury bearing a lunar character in a way. Thus the triad Shamash, Sin, Ishtar, would appear to be analogous with the trinity of principles, astrologically represented by the three heavenly bodies lying within the orbid of the Earth in the solar system: Sun, Mercury, Venus.

Concerning the lunar character of Nebo-Mercury Jastrow in *Die Religion Babyloniens und Assyriens* brings evidence where he treats of Nin-gir-su, which figure appears to bear a resemblance with Ninurta, but principally has to be considered as Mercury. He says then: Next to his martial quality Nin-gir-su had another one, ruled also over agricultural features of the districts. — In this quality he was called Dun-gur or Dun-gur-an, *i.e.* 'god of the corn-heaps'. — A storehouse of victuals is put under his guardianship and an old hymn assimilates him with Tammuz, personification of agricultural activity (RBA, I p. 57/58).

This is comprehensible to astrologers; the cornheaps point to the zodiacal sign Virgo, which is under the rulership of Mercury: Tammuz is the martial feature of the Mid-Summer-expression of the Sun in the zodiacal sign Cancer, *which is ruled by the Moon.*

Another indication is to be found with Jastrow under the name of the god Nusku, a babylonian god probably to be identified with the fire-god Bîl-gi (Gibil) or Girru — in a certain way identified as well with Sin, the lunar god. Ashurbanipal calls him the carrier of the luminous scepter, the same as Nebo is called; anyhow he appears just like this one as the wise god. The two idiomatical symbols of his name, the scepter and the pencil, are united in the person of Nusku as well as in that of Nebo (RBA, I p. 232). The identification of a lunar and a mercurial character seems to be pretty strong here.

In *Babylon, die heilige Stadt* (p. 208) Unger referring to the proper nature of Bēl and quoting Deimel, *Pantheon* No. 2078, p. 173, calls the temple of Bēl the 'house of the day' or of the Sun of the day; consequently his opponent Nabû of Borsippa, the god of the nightly Sun, *i.e.* ruling in the night-time when the Sun is in the underworld, and his temple the house of night.

The evidence is very clear here, as everybody knows that day and night stand in relation to each-other as the Sun and the Moon, consequently Nebo-Mercury is identified with the Moon.

From the list V Rawl. 46 Weidner derives an identification of Nebo with the Moon — though he agrees, that he succeeds only indirectly — by means of the expression Má-Tu, which relates to the crescent Moon, and is used also for Nebo. Therewith the lunar nature of Nebo could be proved sufficiently (HBA, p. 56).

Let us understand that these conceptions, distilled from the numerous documents of ancient Mesopotamia by so many investigators, bear an important evidence and witness of the astral religion or star-lore. Here nothing is inferior to the principles of any other great culture, and in no way. Clearly every part of the happenings in human consciousness is analysed in conformity with the parts of the world's happenings. Such an illustrative analogy has probably never been pronounced so clearly in any other culture in the world.

The question, which Jeremias puts, if the Babylonians at least in later times have known the proper order of the planets within the solar system, is answered by him in the affirmitive, referring to Pythagoras who names them in the order of succession: Moon, Sun, Mercury, Venus, Mars, Jupiter, Saturn; Plato in his *Timaeus* (the same as Aristotle, *de Coelo* II, 12), who gives: Moon, Sun, Venus, Mercury, Mars, Jupiter, Saturn; and Ptolemy: Moon, Mercury, Venus, Sun, Mars, Jupiter, Saturn.

With regard to the latter order of succession I might observe that the spheres around the Earth are meant and that the same must be considered as analogous to the planetary spheres around the Sun (compare EEA, p. 46/47). If we substitute the Sun for the Moon, who in its turn figurates for the planet Earth, as the centre of the earthy spheres, and again the Earth for the Sun, we find, that Ptolemy indeed presents the correct heliocentric order of succession.

The principles, represented by the seven, are illustrated in a good many documents. We refer chiefly to Jastrow, Jeremias, Meissner and Weidner for detailed studies of the same,

Without being able to quote any decided formula in this respect, it appears to me that the functions and qualities of the second triad of gods, Sin, Shamash, Ishtar, as opposites of the fourfoldness Ninurta, Nebo, Nergal, Marduk, and chiefly with regard to the qualities of the four as corner-stones of the cyclic process, are related as subjective *utterances* of consciousness and objective *phases* of consciousness respectively; *i.e.* that they are related in a certain way as the masculine to the feminine or as the creative to the formative or formal side of cosmic happenings in the world's epic of creation. As the three aspects of being — potentiality, ideality, reality, *c.q.* spirit, soul, body — every triad or trinity has to be viewed, in mesopotamian culture as well as elsewhere. The doctrine of Trinity is applicable here (compare EEA). The descriptions earned from the documents prove that one after another the three aspects come to the fore more or less; they prove as well the indestructible unity of the three and the perfectly separate regions ruled by each of them. Primarily, in ancient Ur of the Sumerians, the Moon-god Sin has every attention, he is even called 'Anu', the king and father of the gods, like Anu. He is further called 'the first-born son of Enlil', *i.e.* the elder in the second triad of gods, in whom those who have made a proper study of astrology will immediately understand, that the Lunar Body and lunar being in general preceed the formation of a physical body on Earth as it is built up by the force of the Sun. It does not astonish us to read in this respect that the Moon is the healer, who when neglected causes illness —a conviction, almost shared by our present–time psycho-analysts.

Later, in centuries when the attention of man became more outwardly directed, *e.g.* on conquest of the world and penetration of the babylonian culture and its ritualism by this conquest, the worship of the Moon appears to have dwindled in the background; then lunar life and lunar being has less the attention of men than solar being and its radiant activity, as represented by Marduk principally.

VII. SHAMASH

Shamash is properly and genuinely the god of day and light — Shamash, in Sumerian Utu (the day) and Babbar (the white one), is the manifestation of light in the most extensive sense, particularly the Sun which counted as the greatest planet. From the prayers and hymns to the Sun speaks the immediate sentiment of joy of man longing for light and joy (HAOG, p: 362). The second one of the triad is very evident and naturally the lord of the external world, in which the third, however, representing the aspect of reality or work, will appear as the 'performer' of the heavenly indications. Now the remarkable fact is, that repeatedly we find in the documents Adad or Adad-Ramman as the weather-god, in stead of Ishtar, *i.e.* the god of the earthly atmosphere, by which the earthly phenomena are thought to be ruled or caused, while the more abstract rôle of Venus, angel of light, in these instances remains in the background and appears in another place of mythology. Nevertheless Ishtar remains generally the third of this triad and Adad appears in dayly life as the thunder-god; the latter can be understood now-a-days as the transmitter of the electricity from heaven to earth. Since sumerian times he is also called the son of Enlil, which with regard to the latter cannot be wondered at.

Still all the facts and fancies, c.q. explanations around these cosmic theories are too important and too far reaching to pass them without any further effort to explaining this substitution of one god by another. If the present writer may indulge in a digression on the point: it is not pure amiability to take now and then the Earth instead of Venus, or to call Adad also Venus. Evidently if Adad-Ramman is the thunder-god, son of Enlil, god of the Earth (atmosphere), he yields some power over the Earth. The Earth is always meant and indicated as the third in the trinity at the same time, and the formula comes to be read as Moon-Sun-Earth, which again, if taken in the order Sun-Moon-Earth is an expression for the platonic trinity Spirit-soul-body, as every astrologer knows.

Other planets are now and then called 'son of Enlil' as well, *e.g.* Ningirsu, a mercurial figure sometimes assimilated with Ninurta-Mars, etc. If one understands the language of the astrological mythe, the significance of this title 'Son of Enlil' is evident and clearly this: 'active on the plane of the physical body or in the physical worlds', because Enlil, meaning the Earthgod, is the ruler of the Earth or the physical world. *Lil* means demon. If *demon* is the earthy being, and if the Sun is the symbol of spirit and *deus*, then the Moon is the mediator between demon and deus, body and spirit — which is the actual meaning of the soul. This is one of the many ways of considering the trinity. Perhaps for us, humans, the most important.

Now, in order to understand how it came to pass that in its time Ishtar took the place of Adad-Ramman, we are obliged to recur to the element of the goddess-mother, so very important, in babylonian theology perhaps even more so than the Madonna in the Roman-Catholic doctrine of Christianity.

The scholastic compilers of the gods-lists in the time about 3000 (b.C.) still knew evidently, that the Primeval-Mother — Universal-Mother — transcends all genealogies of the gods. Starting with the triad of divine rulers of this actual world: Anu-Enlil-Ea, they introduced into the midst of it the figure of the Universal Mother, without which no oriental divine worship can be imagined. Her transcendental position above all mythical hierarchic genealogies is apparent from the fact that she is mentioned *without* genealogy, whereas all the other gods are regularly named together wit their genealogy and courtiers. Her figure appears after Anu between Enlil and Ea. The consciousness of the 'eternal feminine' transcending all the gods and belonging to the fundamental state of things, is shown already by the scene of the eagle's flight in the Etana-epic, where above Anu the Madonna is enthroned in the seventh heaven, bearing all human beings, the herb of pregnancy and delivery having to be brougt to the earth thence.

The idea of man being 'the image of the godhead' is again clearly expressed by the Sumerian's assimilation in principle of woman with the universal mother. The sumerian ideogram for priestess consequently is Nin-dingir, *i.e.* 'she who is a ruler devoted to god' (HAOG, p. 333). The Universal Mother is worshipped in Sumer under the name of Ninḫursag, *i.e.* 'ruler of the great (divine) mountain', Ninmaḫ, which means 'powerful ruler', and also, reminding the babbling of the child, Mama or Mami. In the hymns she is called the 'ruler of the gods', 'she who bears the gods', 'who has fed the gods with her holy milk', 'the mother of all men'. She has been called also by the sweet name of Bêlti, 'my ruling goddess', Madonna, 'our beloved lady' (HAOG p, 334).

A direct formula saying that she is symbolised by the Moon, has not been found, but numberless are quotations which indicate her as the partner of the masculin Moon, which could be understood as meaning 'the other side of the lunar nature'. Over and again it is said that the cow pasture and milking are under her direction, as well as agriculture. There are reliefs known indicating this. The astrologer immediately sees that lunar functions are indicated. The symbol for the Moon's crescent attached to the sheepscot must carry the meaning that the male partner of the Universal Mother, worshipped under the symbol of the holy cow, is the Moon, which is imagined as a bull, when the universal Mother figures as a cow (HAOG, p. 335).

The astrologer knows the relationship between the Moon and the sign Taurus. Who studies my *Natural Philosophy* and *Elements* will find that the principle of the Universal Mother indeed covers the sign Taurus *in abstracto* and that every world proceeds from an etheric 'universal mother' or 'etheric matrix'. Evidently such an etheric or abstract (the Hindus say: *arupa)* universal womb is placed higher than every and any concrete active principle of divinity or creative force and that she must have a male partner — to human intelligent understanding — as soon as she (and the human understanding) comes to the scene of 'happenings'. 'Happenings' take place indeed between a 'solar' centre and a 'sphere' or 'lunar' matrix, so much so that 'creation' — which is that what 'happens' — comes forth from the Sun and the

Moon. This third entity in the trinity has been called the Earth, cosmically. Presentday astrology uses the symbols ☉ ☾ ⊕ for these three — like in the most remote times. We shall not enter into further considerations about the fourfold or the threefold of the trinity *plus* the Universal Mother, nor how later-on perhaps the *Tetraktys* might come to be symbol of the four derived from the three *plus* the one-above-all.

The same as with the macro-cosmic triad Anu-Enlil-Ea there is a mother-goddess connected with the cyclic triad, *i.e.* Ishtar (sumerian: Ninni, Ininna). She appears next to Sin, Shamash, Adad-Ramman as a (the) fourth. In the genealogies this 'goddess' appears simply as the daughter of Anu or as the daughter of Enlil (HAOG, p. 336).

Like the Universal Mother it is she who bears all men, 'who makes all creatures prosper'; she is the goddess of love and womanhood. Is she really to be considered — which lies ready at hand — as an analogy of the Universal Mother, particularly with regard to the created (*i.e.* concrete) world, as much as the second divine triad is in dynamical life an analogy of the first triad which is to be thought as static, then she must be seen as the idea-of-the-mother *in concreto* and in all its relations to and in this phenomenal world. Then of course she is "on one hand the priestess of love of the gods, the goddess of the totality of erotic life and birth, . . ." and are we to understand finally how on the other hand she can be understood as 'the ruler of war', because then she actually rules over the whole existence down here, as far as this can be understood as 'the one coming to the other' and as the eternal 'interplay of love and hate', as the Neo-platonists understood it or the war-struggle on *Kurukshetra* as the *Bhagavad Gîta* has it in Indian literature. Jeremias compares her rôle in this respect, and perhaps not incorrectly, with that of a valkyrie, reminding her image in Egyptian mythology, where she is called Hathor and also is represented with cow's horns.

We will meet Ishtar again when treating the planetary principles.

Meanwhile let us try a trifling correction on a saying which appears to me more or less a fallacy — *i.e.* "the serpent is the animal of Ishtar" (HAOG, p. 337). Jeremias illustrates the saying with a small statuette of Ishtar, cherishing a serpent on her breasts. He points to Cleopatra who is known to have taken Ishtar for an example and had herself killed by the bite of a snake in her breasts. Astrologically it does *not* prove that the serpent *rules* the image or the idea or principle of Ishtar, but *opposes* it: astrologically the serpent is the animal of Scorpio, the opposing sign of Taurus, and the example of Cleopatra is a specimen of the law that one (thing or principle) is 'killed' by its 'opponent'. The same principle, referring to the same zodiacal principles or signs can be seen in mithraic images of a bull killed by the bite of a scorpion in the region of the genital parts.

So the divine triad Sin, Shamash, Adad-Ramman is found connected with a fourth principle, Ishtar, but a modification appears to have taken place and Sin, Shamash, Ishtar comes to figure as *the* triad, which by introduction of the lunar character of Nebo-Mercury is to be read as: Sun, Mercury, Venus. These three are then called the rulers of the 'heavenly dam' (HAOG, p, 338).

We know an engraving by Dürer and paintings by Murillo and others, which keep alive a passage in the biblical *Revelation*, where we are told of "a woman clad with the Sun and the Moon being under her feet, bearing on her head a crown of twelve stars" (XII, 1) — the twelve radial starry regions of the 'heavenly dam' or zodiac?

The subsitution of Venus by the Earth, however, appears to carry an other idea and this must have taken place rather early in history, apart from the regular triad Sin, Shamash, Ishtar, which we find on boundary-stones dating as far back as 1350 b. C. (the Sun, the Moon and the eight-pointed star, which is the symbol for Ishtar), as may be seen on a good many boundary-stones in Mesopotamia. The king appears to invoke the aid of the three heavenly powers to protect and to make respect his boundaries.

In esoteric astrology we find Venus as the ruler of the Libra-sphere, meaning the principle which builds the 'body' with the cosmic laws — which are *the* Law. This is explained by her being the transmitter and bearer of the Sun's light — emanation — which creates organic life in all the world; the carrier of light: Lucifer (EEA p. 60). In this way the substitution of the Earth (standing for the principle of *body*) by Venus (representing the inner being or the heavenly side, *i.e.* analogy of the body) may be explained to a certain extent. We shall take leave of the philosophy of trinity now, which certainly deserves a separate treating for which, apart from my own and other astrological works, I might refer to Bhagavan Das' *Science of Peace.*

On the other hand we find the four: Marduk (Jupiter), Ninurta (Mars), Nebo (Mercury), Nergal (Saturn). How or in what way we have to understand that these four rule the corners of the cyclic process — seasons, Moon's quarters, the Sun's daily positions, *e.t.q.* — I have not found in any of the works based upon the available documents. The question has perhaps not been put by these researchers who were little or nothing in the way of an astrologer, to whom the 'reason why' must naturally appeal.

The cyclic process, being the *procédé* of everything that happens in Nature and that which consequently human consciousness has to go through, is the objective side of the coming to consciousness. Now this must — astrologically speaking — find itself represented in the objective side of the solar system (EEA, chapt. IV says the objective side of the solar half of the solar system), the subjective side consisting of the Sun, Mercury, Venus, the heavenly bodies in the system on the centre-side as seen from the Earth. This objective side shews us the planets Mars, Jupiter, Saturn. In Saturn — taken as a phase, stage or category — the process of coming to consciousness begins: birth of concrete consciousness. In Nature this category is represented by the mineral kingdom and particularly by the crystal. Thus astrologically the midwinter-point is the birth-moment in the solar cycle of the year and is ruled by Saturn-Nergal. Consciousness expands and the middle of the phase of growth is reached in that cycle at the moment of the Sun passing the equator; therefore the vernal equinox was said to be ruled by Jupiter-Marduk, the planet of growth and emanation. The faculty of growth is coming to existence in the vegetal kingdom. The third stage is that of the culmination or the end of growth. Growth is consumed — mathematically. And that which has been grown in the vegetal kingdom will be consumed by another category of creatures, constituting the animal kingdom and symbolised by Mars-Ninurta. In the cycle of consciousness it means the conversion of outer into inner consciousness; it is the turningpoint of the orientation of consciousness. This means the animal stage which is that of consuming, but which includes and compels the fourth, *i.e.* presupposes the human stage. In the midsummer-point the vegetal expression of the 'solar heros' is killed by the animal. This has been told in the mythe of Tammuz-Adonis, who was killed by a boar. The fourth stage in the cyclic process of the year is that of the autumnal equinox in which the decreasing light symbolises the course of the solar heros through the underworld, *i.e.* life and its now converted consciousness returning to Self, its centre. It of course symbolises the journey of the Spirit — being called the pilgrim — through the world of matter, and all this must undoubtedly have been the matter of all solar myths and of the babylonian in the first place. Even so if the Earth, in those old myths and cosmogonies, did not figurate as a planet and the solar system was not presented as helio-centric — about which nothing indeed can be found. The fourth stage — continuing present-day astrological considerations — takes place on the planet Earth, or is symbolised by this heavenly body's place in the solar system. To indicate this stage in the cycle of consciousness — the human stage after the animal kingdom, a stage quite apart — the planet is represented by its Moon and finally the latter is compared with, and supplanted by, Mercury-Nebo, which is standing to the Sun about the same as our Moon to our Earth — astrologically as well — *i.e.* like a watcher or ruler of an 'etheric matrix' or 'motherly sphere' stands to the centre. Thus Mercury-Nebo came to indicate and rule the fourth stage in the cycle of consciousness and every other cycle; the stage of mankind, which, after that of the animal, is the stage of work; work again means: descending into the underworld, into matter, in order to come to know matter. This 'proceeding of descent' is the typical expression for the birth of spiritual man in this world of phenomenal being and embodiment — common to all lines of expressing the mystical or inner side of life.[1])

Nebo conducts the solar heros back to the midwinterpoint, which consequently gets a second meaning, *i.e.* that of the 'second birth', rebirth or spiritual birth in human consciousness. And in the myths and legends the cyclic process of the apparent course of the Sun around the Earth is the pattern of the pilgrimage of cosmic life and human consciousness in particular through *the* World.

It is said that Nebo takes over the function of *mediator* from his father Marduk — which saying is hardly to be understood when taking the names as indicating the planets, but may appear very clear when one considers both of them as principles in the cyclical process and as partial expressions of the solar power, and the one as 'taking over' the duty of the other — meaning: doing the opposite function.

Thus Nebo takes over from Marduk the office of mediator. Perhaps the functioning as such by both of them may be understood in connection with their ruling the equinoctial points of the annual cycle. Ungnad's comment runs: "In how far the christian representation of the Son's Mediator's rôle, without whom nobody comes to the Father, is founded upon ancient oriental thought, we will not investigate here" (RBAU, p. 10).

The death of Tammuz-Adonis is bewailed by his 'beloved' Ishtar, who followed him into the underworld and not only mourns him there, but takes all pains to deliver him from his emprisonment and thereto engages herself in battle against the feminine partner of Nergal. This mythical tale is worth mentioning, because it partly explains at the same time another myth, *i.e.* that of Saturn-Nergal descending into the underworld and becoming 'lord of the dark side' and 'god of the region of death'. — The tale of Nergal's descent into hell explains how from the original solar god Nergal became a prince of darkness and the partner of Ereshkigal (Meissner, BA, II, p. 184).

This Ereshkigal, originally the goddess and ruler of the underworld or kingdom of darkness, is a remarkable image of the idea — evidently existing among the Sumerians already — that woman rules the dominion of darkness and the night. She sends a messenger, called Namtaru, to the council of the gods, but Nergal is wanting in respect towards him, which means towards his principal, by not rising from his seat, and Ereshkigal to avenge the wronging summons him to her kingdom. Nergal descends to fight her, he conquers Namtaru and afterwards Ereshkigal herself, after which in tears she begs to become his wife: he himself, Nergal, would become Lord of the Underworld by that. Nergal kisses her and takes her unto him: — symbolising the 'fall' of the Angel by 'descending' into the dark domain of woman and accepting her, the more strikingly illustrated in this myth by the saying that it was caused by 'the wanting in respect for the woman'. Of course the meaning is: Ereshkigal 'seduces' Nergal and causes in him a loss of respect, in order to have claim upon him, inducing him further to conquer her: a conquest which enslaves him. "Thus the antagonistic couple comes to peace and forthwith rules the underworld." (Meissner). Apparently this is a 'formula' and of exactly as much and nearly the same meaning as „*alle Schuld rächt sich auf Erden*", — to be read with the accent on the last word in both cases. Not only here in this instance descriptions in myths and legends have the value of cosmical formulas. Sometimes when the formulas are well understood we may work with them. So if we say: Nergal becomes the ruling power of the kingdom of darkness, which is at the same time the kingdom of the physical form, it means conversely the god or angel or divine consciousness in the condition of darkness or 'form', etc.

The next stage is the promoting to the function or 'lord' of that world ruled by woman, *i.e.* the world of the physical formation as proceeding from woman, the world also which comes forth from the 'etheric matrix', so much so that Nergal-Saturn

---

[1]) The fact that there are certain species in the animal kingdom — beavers, ants, termites, bees, wasps — that show the development of working and building capacities wholly serviceable to the community and in this respect even surpassing man, does not deny that work is the specific task of the human stage — compare *Genesis* III, 19.

has become the Lord of the Form or bodily existence. A law in astrology known to every astrologer now, though no longer presented in so poetic a version. (Compare EEA, Chapt. V)

Returning to the myth of Tammuz-Adonis:

The cycle of human consciousness, as illustrated by the apparent course of the Sun round the Earth, truly of the Earth round the Sun, is not the experience of the Most High (consciousness) in Itself, but that of "God's Son", who was called Tammuz in Babylon, in sumerian: Dumu-zi; later on in hellenistic times Adonis, in Greece Dionysos, in Rome Bacchus. The sumerian name means 'veritable (or legal?) son', from which 'solar child' becomes clear. In the saga Tammuz is represented as an ancient king on earth who won great fame as a 'fisher' and a 'hunter'. Although the explanations which I venture to offer are not to be found in Meissner's work, which is quoted, my conclusions appear to be justified by the quotations. Thus: fame as a fisher and a hunter will morally, not be far from meaning the conquests of human consciousness on the animal — an attainment which is taught in almost every system of ethics. "In his youth he was lying in a ship immersed in the water" — "when grown up he was embedded and lying in the corn" —, Theosophically and astrologically it illustrates the fact of the soul primarily incarnating in an etheric or 'lunar' body, in the region of 'the waters', and afterwards only coming to full development in the physical world where there is sawing and reaping; embedded means incarnated, I should like to read.

In the heat of summer, in the month of Tammuz, called after him, he disappears from the Earth and passes the western plain to the underworld ... the reason for the departure of Tammuz can not yet be indicated by us with certainty ... says Meissner (BA, II, p. 25) We cannot ascertain as yet whether it were Ishtar, the beloved of his youth, who destroys him with her hot love and causes him to be bewailed year after year, or, like a later saga has it, a boar who kills him. In relating this epic Meissner does not touch the probable cosmic meaning of it, at least there is no allusion to it. But still: After his departure ... after 'his disappearance from the land', he is, apparently, not dead for ever but, together with his comrade Nigishzida [1]) resides in the underworld during part of the year ... In order to liberate her lover, Ishtar rendered herself into Hades [2]) and after endless difficulties and dangers she succeeds in the venture and brings him back into the upperworld ... — then plants and animals become fertile again ... "fertility and growth reappear ..." (BA, II, p. 25)

The epic of Ishtar's descent into hell is the dramatic scene of man's experience of a cosmic and mystic happening, *i.e.* that of going through the 'lower' half of himself. A simile singularly rich in significance and apt to be dramatised. We cannot help finding a certain resemblance between the liberation of Tammuz-Adonis from the Kingdom of Ereshkigal who falls in love with him and tries to keep him with her ('down'), by the rescuing act of Ishtar-Venus, goddess of love, and the germanic saga of Tannhäuser, who could only be freed from the spell, which caught him in the cave of Venns, and brought to a new life, by the pure love of a woman. Only the remarkable fact is, that the later version of the myth evidently knew of no other name for the magic spell of physical attraction than 'Venus'. It might have been a different name. Remarkable as well is, in the later version the idea of rebirth, indicated as it is by the re-budding of Tannhäuser's staff. In the Tannhäuserlegend the nature of woman is dualistic — there is a side of magic spell and lust and that of liberating love — like in the ancient sumerian-babylonian myth.

The general sagas and epic tales of the Sumerians, handed over to babylonian culture as a rule, bear a very interesting cosmic significance most of them, which can be immediately transfered into functions of human life, into phases of human consciousness and evolution of soul and body. Strictly speaking the morals and ethics derived from this system of great cosmic examples must be of the purest nature, not only poetic and

---

1) Another name for Mercury-Nebo; compare 'consciousness' in EEA and N. Ph.

2) This has been astronomically explained by the passing of the Sun together with the planets Mercury and Venus through the winter half of the year.

romantic, but of an extraordinarily theological and philosophical virtue. This may be stated here emphatically in contradiction to those who maintain that mesopotamian culture — and evidently so on account of its later outgrowths and Christianity's superiority over these — was no more than a 'heathen belief' of a low order and its astrology a make-believe. All problems of ethics — as treated by christian doctrine with regard to the salvation of profane man from his delusion, his being ensnared in conceit and selfdeceit, very often finds a parallel in one of the epics of that ancient civilisation apparently.

Is there one great culture known up to the present days, in which the supreme power in nature as exerted by the Sun has not given rise to divine worship? Very much on the surface it lies in the babylonian culture, where the Sun is lord of the world of Nature or physical existence. This natural solar worship praised so highly by Goethe, has passed with its symbolism not only into Hellenism, into the gnostic heathen church, but as well into Christianity, which conquered it. — Saying 'Christ is the Sun' is more than a comparison (HAOG, p. 362 footnote).

The Sun is praised, which moves daily in its course over sea and land, along Earth and Heaven and at night below the sea so as to view also the monsters of the waters, nay, be able to guard the underworld with its ghosts of the dead. — The Sun makes everything come to light (HAOG, p. 362).

It will be clear how in the solar religion and worship the solar idea is the polar opposite but even therefore coupled to the lunar idea in lunar worship and religion.

The divine worship of the Sun and the Moon appeared next to one another since the most remote times (HAOG, p. 367).

The principal sites of this worship were at Lagash, Larsa and Sippar. Jastrow writes in this relation: In Ur itself Shamash was worshipped beside the Moon in early days already (ca. 2800 b.C.), there is also a temple consacrated to the two together.

The usual symbol for the Sun is a circle or round disc with a fourpointed star inscribed in it and four sheaves or rays at midways between the four points of the star, indicating eight directions in total.

Important is the observation made by Jastrow, that the public worship done in the name of Shamash, appears to be founded on his position as dependent from the lunar god (RBA, p. 66). If the sun is to be seen in the first place as the ruler of physical life, and *before* this the Moon is the ruler of abstract or etheric life in the Universe, then the said conviction of the Babylonians denotes a very high standard of cosmic philosophy. *i.e.* that abstract or etheric life is to be considered of primary importance, the physical concreteness only as secondary. Nevertheless the Sun or the solar principle is in this world of matter the 'god of light', who is invoked 'to banish darkness and avert calamnity', also the 'king of judgment' and his activities are generally considered as beneficial. He is alternatively king and shepherd. It is said that the title shepherd was introduced by the people of semitic origin, descending from the arabian desert plateau into the plain and who originally were shepherd-tribes, a reason also for calling stars and planets 'sheep', but this is not denying that these peoples connected an as much symbolic meaning and even a spiritual one with the word shepherd as others did with 'king'.

The solar god sits on his throne as the judge, 'superior judge of the underworld' and it is he who is 'able to loosen the chains of the prisoners and to give back life to the dead'.

The definition as 'superior judge of the underworld' reminds us of Osiris in the *Book of the Dead* — Pluto in Greece — who is lord of the 'underworld' and who actually delivers judgment on mortals wishing to leave this (sub-lunar) world for an existence in heavenly regions, which must be interdicted to those who are still burdened and heavy (at heart) by carrying the remembrances of the world of earth. They must be light like a feather, and therefore the latter is weighed in the balance against the candidate's heart — astrologically the heart is ruled by the Sun. Thus the lord of the Sun, being the lord of the heart as well, sits in judgment over this (under-)world. Verily a moral dictment of no mean virtue. There are a good many Shamash-texts reminding the relation between this divine principle and the region of death, *i.e.* the underworld. It is actually the whole existence in the physical body — the 'sub-lunar' world — which has been called the 'underworld' — and thus by mystics of all ages and peoples. This fact must be borne in mind because it explains the seeming contradiction between the praising of the Sun's light and life-giving force, *versus* the presiding over the 'regions of death'. The one regards profane life in this world, the other is related to the life of the soul. The solar god is not only the god of the day and life, but he also eyery day treads the underworld and in this way is the ruler of the dead as well as of the living — 'judge of the upper- and the under-world' — which astronomically of course points to the upper- and the lower-meridian transits of the Sun at midday and midnight.

The comparison with Osiris is a liberty which I take here and I even might extend it to the rôle of Mediator which Christ plays in Christianity where he is said to be born at midnight and midwinterpoint, afterwards to be the judge of men.

Jastrow continues: His light was a symbol of probity the wanting of it, darkness, counted as godlessness (RBA, p. 69).

In countries where the climate causes the Sun to be not only and always pleasant and beneficial in relation to human, physical conditions, the Moon is very often viewed as friendly, but the Sun as inimical with its scorching heat (HAOG, p. 362, footnote). Sometimes the Sun is called the 'physician' like the Moon. This has been explained by some as an indication of the mixing of the population with elements from a cooler climate. Of course such considerations are only taking into account exoteric elements. Still there is so much of polarity and cosmic relationship to be found in these solar and lunar worshippings, which are so close parallels, that even Jeremias' saying: Real mystic motives are few in solar worship (HAOG, p. 365, footnote), makes us wonder a little why he did not see the inner qualities as well. The same with a lecturer at the congress of the Netherland's *Oostersch Genootschap* at Leiden in 1933, who ventured the verdict: "Of mysticism there is nothing to be found in it at all".

Still, there is truth in the verdict, and Sun-worship very often becomes exoteric and materialistic. Modern astrology knows why. The star-lists worked out by Weidner in his *Astronomie* contain some remarkable material with regard to certain relations between the Pleiades and Hyades, sometimes the star Aldebaran, short the constellations in and about the Bull (*kakkab* Dilgan, also Ku Mal (= Hun-Gá) and *kakkab* Zappu). A particular scene in the babylonian tableau of the calendar is the conjunction of the Pleiades with the Moon says Weidner (HBA, p. 170). And from starlist 17 Br. M. 86378 IV 33: The *kakkab* Zappu is called the first among 'lunar mansions'. This predilection is in agreement with the important rôle played by the Pleiades in Babylon. With the Indians the Kṛittikâ (Pleiades) count as the first lunar station as well. Narrow relations between babylonian and indian astronomy having moreover been established (compare Kugler) there can hardly be any more question about the indian lunar stations being deduced from Babylon originally (HBA, p. 173).

Now astronomy has since calculated — by means of observing and measuring the proper motions of stars — that the star group of the Pleiades — if not the centre of the universe — must about indicate the centre of a very large starry system, the milky way of which our solar system is part. So much so that our Sun plays a rather subordinante rôle with regard to the Pleiades. Had our babylonian predecessors in astronomy such an enormous vision of real relations in the heavens that they understood this? It is hardly to be answered at present. But astrologically they must have known. They may have understood the *Bilderbuch* of the starry heavens better than intricate calculations. If the Pleiades were granted to be the centre of a much larger system than our solar system, then a proportional greater soul might be expected to have its central seat there, practically representing a power to which *our* solar system has been proved to be subordinated, physically and why not psychically?

Starlists II R. 49,3 and II R. 51,2. 58—71 considered as very important ones mention *kakkab* GU-AN-NA as 'Heavenly Bull' (Taurus), the Hyades, Aldebaran; *kakkab* SIB-ZI-AN-NA as 'the faithful shepherd of heaven'.

The Bull and Orion appear always together. Hellenistic times have rendered it distinctly (Weidner HBA, p. 31).

So there possibly is a certain analogy existing between Orion and the Sun, as a shepherd? If so the Babylonians must have grasped a great idea with regard to the structure of the heavenly systems.

Speaking of the second divine triad in comparison with the first, Jastrow says: This second group stands in a higher esteem in Babylon than in Assyria, and though it only appears more emphatically in the texts of the second period, it must be granted to be formulated already by the general acknowledgment of Marduk's supremacy (RBA, p. 258). The latter is perhaps not a direct indication, but we have to accept Marduk as the upper god for Babylon and a good deal of the countries where babylonian culture reigned. Never Sin or Shamash is mentioned as such and no more Anu: Marduk is the lord and leader of the gods and the protector of the entire cultus and culture. He stands like Zeus with the Greeks. Zeus or Marduk however are not the personification of the planet in the first place but of the Sun in the vernal equinox and of the Sun rising in the East, *i.e.* the solar power going to dominate the outer world. This appears to indicate how much the terrestrial power and regency of the planets, Sun and Moon *in concreto* is meant in the saga and legends of babylonian culture *after all* and how evidently the heavenly powers *in abstracto* remain behind the veil. It is impossible, however to continue this apreciation into a more concise theory about lower and higher principles — the less so as — like Jastrow states it "the origin of babylonian literature is conceiled in darkness".

There is peculiar interchanging, *i.e.* that of the significances and functions of Mercury-Nebo and Ninib-Ninurta, which can be either Mars or Saturn. In the list Br. M. 86378 the god Mash is mentioned and Weidner makes the following annotation: this is a phenomenal expression of Ninib in the same way as several places give the assimilation of Ninib and Mercury — Mercury whose name is Ninib (HBA, p. 42) No lay-man could ever find the way out. One can say: Mercury is the 'binder', Saturn is the one that was 'bound'. Then the question may be put: is the 'binder' at the same time the one that was bound — in the way of causing himself to be bound — by desire *e.g.* — as Rabindranath Tagore puts it so well and poetic in his *Gitanjali* "...Prisoner, who was it that bound thee?..." etc. and the christian Gospel of St. Mathew apparently makes the same understand in Chapt. V, 26.

The chief god revealing himself in the planet Mercury is Nebo, god of the West and the autumnal point.

Both gods, Nebo and Mash, agree in their astral characters; with regard to the definition of the manysided gods' revelation this fixing of the identity is important (HBA, p. 42).

Mercury is also called 'the planet planet' — planet *par excellence*? Anyhow it is the first planet which appears next to the Sun, opening the chain of planets, consequently starting the idea or principle of the 'planetary' (compare EEA).

Another hint at the relation of Mercury-Nebo with Ninib-Ninurta meant as Mars is to be found in the list V R. 46, where on the one hand Saturn-Jupiter and on the other Mars-Mercury are called 'twin planet'. The meaning is evident: Saturn-Nergal is the principle of concentration, condensation, etc. etc., Jupiter-Marduk indicates the opposite faculties and qualities: expansion, sublimation, etc. etc. In the same way the strongly outgoing energy of Mars-Ninurta could be regarded as the opposite quality of Mercury-Nebo's reduction into inner being. This follows from the year's cyclic process. Every astrologer knows it.

A propos of this list Weidner says: Apparently the different schools of astrologers in Babylon followed different traditions.

Still the different traditions, though seemingly contradictory, may be found to relate to the inherent characters of the gods, *i.e.* cosmic principles on one of their different stages of working.

VIII. SIN

Sin was called EN-ZU in sumerian, or also ZU-EN, which abbreviated would have given Sin; in Akkadian it reads Nannar, a male god whose female partner (or side?) was called Ningal or Nikkal, 'the great ruler', who 'together with him in the heavens decides the decrees of fate' and is considered to be the mother of the solar god (HAOG, p. 355—360), so much so that the male character (or side?) leaves no doubt whatever. From the indications of the female side of the lunar being we may conclude that the etheric matrix is the idea in the cosmical sense therefrom deriving all intimation in the direction of womanhood and motherhood *in concreto* — a miraculous height of knowledge of the ancient Babylonians. The indication 'mother of the solar god' can hardly relate to the Earth's Moon, but only to a cosmic being or principle of a much higher nature. The 'female' nature of it must necessarily allude to its being abstract or etheric towards the so said positive or masculine nature of the concrete physical world (compare my N. Ph. and EEA).

In the ancient hymns of Ur, where he is worshipped originally as the highest deity, the lunar god is called also 'king' and 'father' of the gods, like Anu. There is also a place where he is called 'the first born son of Enlil' who cosmically is the deity of heavenly as well as of the earthy Earth (-element), with which he corresponds in the cyclic doctrine (HAOG, p. 336). The particular attention paid to the lunar god at Ur is historically known to date from about 3000 b.C., when the vernal equinox passed through the constellation of the Bull, consequently coïncides with the appearance of the Bull image in religion and architecture. Present-day astrology still says the Moon is 'exalted' in Taurus.

He is praised as a 'merciful father' and in hymns is said that 'his word makes that foods and drinks thrive; 'fills the stable and sheepscot'.

Therefore the Moon is also the physician, which becomes apparent from certain proper names — says Jeremias. The principles of father and mother being brought together in the lunar nature, which means: the etheric abstract going together with the physical or concrete, is apparent from a song to be found in list IV R. 9, where 'the merciful, gracious father Nannar' is said to make his appearance 'as a bull so young and strong and with powerful horns'; and again, with regard to his phases, which contain the mystery of life and death, as fruit which produces itself from itself (and always anew) and grows, divine to look at, the fruit on the opulence of which one can never satisfy oneself; mother's womb, which bares every being... merciful father in whose hand the life of the whole country is lying (HAOG, p. 361, 362).

A very remarkable annotation is made by Jeremias:

Above all the Moon has procured the best material for a perception of the doctrine of Saviours. One sees how every month — the Babylonians call him admiringly the fruit which produces itself from itself anew — he is born mysteriously, he grows ever stronger and finally conquers the dark power (the black Moon), who had consumed him. In the Full Moon he has his summit of ruling power, which, however, is at the same time the critical turningpoint (therefore in the myth wedding is analogous with death). He dies gradually, encompassed by the dark power, until for three days he takes rest to rise conquering and be greeted again with jubilation in his new light (crescent) (HAOG, p. 357).

Jastrow brings an indication with regard to the mediatorship of the Moon:

As the Moon, in consequence of the regularity of its change of light, gives much more guidance to mankind than the Sun, the religious systems brought him into relation with the forces of heaven as well as with those of the Earth.

The ideograms for Sin indicate him as being considered as the 'lord of wisdom'. The ideas of wisdom and light not standing far apart, it is particularly Sin, however, who appears as the 'distributor of light' (RBA, p. 75).

Jastrow says also, that the divine character of Sin as a godhead does not appear so emphatically as that of the other gods, from which it would result that this nature lies more in a general sphere.

Now we may conceive a certain polarity or contrast between the worshipping in the one line and along the other: the solar worship puts up an other ideal than the lunar worship. Hellenistic considerations about the moments of the Full Moon and the New Moon confirm that there are two opposite quests: which reminds of the English saying "*you can 't burn the candle both ends*". There is the ideal of wordly success, well-being and happiness (Sun); and there is, on the other hand, the ideal of spiritual development and consciousness: which includes every religious idea (Moon). Conciliation appears to the possible. The two categories, contrarious as they are, must finally be brought together and united in mankind. The means of this uniting, the relation between the two is offered by Ishtar.

This divine triad — not to be considered only or chiefly as a 'trinity' or tri-unity — has to be viewed from different points of view. Thus Jeremias relates that Sun and Moon were considered as 'enemy-brothers', whose paths went different ways, while otherwise Sun and Moon were called the 'great twins'. Very often Tiâmat (chaos) was represented by the Moon (reminds the sign Cancer), *i.e.* as a power of evil, while Marduk represents the chief quality for the good in the Sun: as raising and healing.

A very important view on the duality Sun-Moon is that of marriage-partners, and the obscuration of the Moon from the Sun's light is represented preferentially as a solar disc closely surmounting a lunar sickle, which is practically described as 'sleeping in one bed', while Venus is then pictured as a star standing at the side. In the vocabulary says Jeremias, the 'with each other' is also to be understood as 'in each other'. This idea and the picturing of it in so many places clearly appears to relate to the function of Ishtar as the bond that unites (the two). I have not yet found this explanation in one of the works of our learned commentators, but I should like to emphasize it even. In symbolic language we very often find the power, which causes a certain happening or fact, pictured together with that fact in one combination or an other. This is universal. We find it in egyptian as well as in babylonian and assyrian symbolism. The image of Ishtar next to this 'marriage' of the Sun and the Moon evidently means, after this rule of symbolism, that the marriage is concluded by Ishtar, or that Ishtar 'rules' marriage, as an astrologer would put it, *i.e.* the uniting of polar opposites.

IX. ISHTAR

The former leads to an other image *i.e.* of Ishtar as the child of the two, which, however, is not expressed literaly, as far as I know, but is found separately in definitions such as 'daughter of Anu' (Gilgamesh epic), 'daughter of Ea', as well as it might be considered to lie concealed in all such names which describe either the solar or the lunar nature of Ishtar.

It has been asked whether the Babylonians have known already the 'horns', *i.e.* the phases of Venus; which would look probable in the great work on *omina* (HAOG, p. 172). They knew certainly that Venus appears either as the morningstar or as evening star. The fact that its brilliant light remained visible in the morning after that of the other heavenly bodies had faded, and became visible in evening twilight before any other star, says Jeremias, may have been the reason for calling Venus the star *par excellence.*

The acknowledging of the Morningstar and the Eveningstar to be one and the same has been proved mythologically by the texts from Nineveh, *i.e.* by calling Venus in the West, that is as Eveningstar, the feminine Venus, and in the East, as Morningstar, the masculine Venus. This mythological splitting up is the same that has been taken over by the Greeks later on where they make a distinction between their Madonna Athene as a goddess of war and Aphrodite, goddess of love. The masculine 'Morningstar deity' is always the warlike, the feminine Eveningstar the goddess of love in the sense of Eros (HAOG, p. 170). This explains the remarkable thing in the viewing of the Assyrians about Ishtar, whose protection in war they invoke and wherewith her image is lacking altogether in sweet or loveable qualities of the other side. Every astrologer nowadays knows that the venusian sign of the zodiac Libra in its constructive mental ways and diplomatical gestures is very cold and impassive, domineering and crual. This apparently was known as well to the ancient Assyrians, warlike as their nature was.

Furthermore we have to see Ishtar as the mother-goddess Ninni (Innanna), which now and again interchanges with the picture of the virgin with the ears of corn. The ears of corn in connection with the image of the mystery of life and death can be seen as the death and life of the grain of seed, like we found it proved for Babylonia (p. 339) and like it has been pictured in hellenistic days in the Eleusinian mysteries (HAOG, p. 171).

A hymn from the temple archives of Nippur written in classical sumerian, shews the starry madonna to recede into sumerian time.

Ishtar is the prominent star, *i. e.* the Great Mother of the gods, the Madonna descended into the world of physical reality: phenomenon of a cosmic or abstract noumenon. [1]) As to the 'virgin with the child' symbol a very remarkable communication is made by Jeremias, quoting material given by Boll in his *Sphaera* p. 512. etc.: The arabian scientist Abu Ma'sar refering to Teukros the learned Babylonian, gives a symbolic description of each decanate of the twelve zodiacal signs in its rise (ascendant). Of the first decanate of the Virgin (Virgo) is said... a Virgin called Isis by Teukros; she is a beautiful pure young woman with long hair, sweet of looks; she carries two ears of corn in her hand and is seated on a throne on which lie pillows. She guards a boy and feeds him with pap, in a place called Atrium; this boy is called Isu (Jesus) by some pleoples (HAOG, p. 172).

The semitic origin of the name (Ishtar) is no longer disputed seriously by any scientist. The root shews etymological relationship with the god Ashur. If this be the case, Ishtar could signify 'the goddess who brings blessing', but this is all as dubious as a good many other etymologies that have been proposed (Jastrow, RBA, footnote p. 81).

The same author relates the qualities of Venus under the name of Bau or Babu — perhaps the most prominent goddess of ancient babylonian history — Bau is the 'mother of the gods' — In the ancient babylonian inscriptions she is called the principal daughter of Anu, god of heaven (RBA p. 58). She is the 'merciful ruler'... who disposes the vicissitudes of mankind and procures plenty to the plougher of the soil. She is the one who fills with reason. (RBA, p. 59) She is the goddess of Lagash and most of the relative documents are found there.

This goddess, 'the wife of Ningirsu', who also wielded power over Lagash, has been connected with marriage presents. As the wife of Ningirsu she is identical with the goddess Gula, who generally appears as the 'royal wife of Ninib' (Ninurta) and whose worship is kept up till in the New-Babylonian Kingdom.

Jastrow means: Bau is Gula as well as, and because Ningirsu is Ninurta.

For the rest it is certain that Bau originally was an independent goddess — that she counts as the 'daughter of Anu'. From these definitions it is clear that the sumerian and ancient babylonian goddess Bau was really Venus. The same definitions are given, later, for Ishtar.

In general Ishtar is *not* to be considered as the 'wife', however, — says Jastrow — because her characteristic quality is her independent position, her substantial nature. Not as only a reflexion of a masculine deity, although she may be called sometimes 'the beloved spouse of Ashur' (RBA, p. 218).

She is the only goddess to appear in the assyrian pantheon. On a single occasion,

[1]) Compare also Ungnad; Weidner *Astronomie*; Virolleaud *Ishtar* I, 5, 6, 10.

i.e. by Ashurbanipal, she has been called Ashuritu, which means *the* goddess, being more of an honorific title than something of the nature of 'wife' dependent on Ashur, albeit that she appears at his side (RBA, p. 214). The latter of course relates to the Ishtar of the town Ashur, wife of the god of that name, as distinguished from the Ishtar of Nineveh, Arbela, etc.

A certain connection between the Venus-figure and Ea is indicated, but we will not lose ourselves in it here, because it would ask too much cosmological explanation. That which is offered by Jastrow does not look altogether satisfying.

In early babylonian and sumerian days a relation is still evident between ideas about the Moon and Venus, *i.e.* in the names Innina (Innanna) and Ninâ or Nanâ, the first name also shortened as Ninni. To Gudea Innina is the 'ruler of the world' and 'the ruler of battle' — as these goddesses both represented the same principles of generation and fertility, they were conjoined quite naturally, at the uniting of the babylonian states, to one great mother-goddess. — who was generally called Nanâ or Ishtar. King Rim-Sin of Larsa calls Innina 'the daughter of Sin'. In the fully developped cosmology Innina appears as the planet Venus, whose differrent phases as Morning- and Evening-star caused a comparison with the phase of the Moon to be male quite naturally (RBA, p. 77).

About the ideogram Ninâ or Nanshe Jastrow adds, that it means the 'house of the fish'. Modern astrology knows the relation of Venus with the zodiacal sign Pisces, in which sign the planet is said to be 'exalted'.

The same ideogram has been used for the town Nineveh, which properly ought to be written Ni-nu-a. Nineveh was called 'the beloved town of Ishtar'. The identity is very clear here.

Calling Ishtar the 'ruler of the countries' and the 'ruler of the moutains' would be quite sufficient to justify the relation of Venus with the earthy sign Taurus, as is well known in astrology, and which zodiacal sign has to do with the country, with agriculture, as well as Capricorn, which sign also rules mountains.

X. THE QUATERNARY

NERGAL-SATURN

Then, after the dynamic or motoric divine triad Sin, Shamash, Adad — Moon, Sun, Earth — appears the 'planetary fourfoldness' Marduk, Ninurta, Nebo, Nergal, which represents the four cardinal phases or cornerpoints of the cycle and of cyclic happening: Jupiter, Mars, Mercury, Saturn.

"Each one of the four (planets) bears a solar character, however, in which Marduk reveals his power particularly in the morning- and springtime Sun, Nabu (Nebo) in the evening- and autumn-Sun, Ninurta in the noon- and summer-Sun, Nergal in the low-sunken Sun in winter, like it has descended into the underworld at midnight also, to assert itself in the morning, like in the winter tropic, as the 'unconquered Sun'" (HAOG, p. 191).

Remarkable is the interchanging of Nergal and Ninurta in some places. In the star lists and omina texts, as treated by Weidner, this interchange is to be found in several instances. For the rest this case is no more strange than the mixing up of the significances of the 'devil' and 'satan' in our modern diction: again representatives of Mars and Saturn repectively. Perhaps a good many Christians are even so totally unaware of any difference between the two, using the names the one for the other without any preference whatever. Kugler, in his *Sternkunde und Sterndienst* of 1907 states: it is undeniable truly, that the deities Nin-Ib (= Ninurta) and Nergal are hardly distinguishable from one another in the religious texts. — He adds: only it does not follow that the names of the *planets*, to which these deities were addicted, participated in the interchange; it even appears impossible in the cases where the name of the planet expressed its being (SSB, p. 220). In the starlist V R. 46 (Weidner

HBA, p. 55) we find a specimen of the same: Ninurta is called Summer-solstice *and* Saturn; Nergal identified with the winter-solstice *and* Mars. Still this must be understood as a mistake or misrepresentation, because astrologically it can be reasoned, that the midwinterpoint indicates the nature of Saturn as shrinking, condensation, cristallisation, concentration, lower meridian, death, etc. — and not that of Mars (energy pointed outward). This cannot be a mistake of Weidner himself, but must lie in the text, evidence of which gets confirmation from other places in the same list.

Jeremias cannot find a way out of the intricacies apparently, where he is trying to explain the cross of the four winds and seasons together with the names of the four planetary principles (HAOG, p. 185), stating about 'Nergal-Mars', and 'Ninib or Ninurta-Saturn'... "The principal direction South, as taken astronomically, becomes a cosmical direction North". (?) In what way we may try to interprete this, one thing is certain, *i.e.* that South never will be North and that only certain names placed at the corners may change. The difference between 'astronomically' and 'cosmically' moreover is rather arbitrary, but even if the idea was to distinguish the orientation on Earth from that in the heavens, then even North remains North and South remains South. His conclusion "we see in this scheme the explanation for the planets of North and South being able to change their rôles, without the planets themselves doing so"... does not explain anything at all, as far as I see. Even when, like mentioned in a footnote, Jensen acknowledges the Saturn-significance of Ninurta and Thompson chooses to call Nergal also Mars, the matter does not become any the more clear. Neither does it when astrologers come to aid by stating that Mars is exalted in the saturnian sign Capricorn. There is and there must be of course a cosmological, *i.e.* astrological, explanation, why these two functions are being mixed up so very often as to confuse the expressions in human consciousness called Mars and Saturn.

Jeremias does not get out of the riddle and one cannot get out, because two different cycles are mixed up: the year's cycle, having its lowest decline in the midwinterpoint — on our northern hemisphere the coldest point — lying in the South, the northern culmination in midsummer being the warmest; on the contrary the day's cycle has its higher culmination together with the warmest moment of the day at noon in the South, and the lower culmination together with the coldest point at midnight in the North. If viewed in this way, we may come to understand why at one time Saturn is indentified with the North (midnight) and at another with the South (midwinter); and the reverse with Mars.

Still this does not explain anything about the interchange of the functions of Mars and Saturn: categorically they are perfectly different. Astrologically-cosmologically the two cycli are as much different: the day's cycle is that which is described by the Earth around its own axis and in which the planet is itself the centre; this bestows on this cycle a value of centrality, *i.e.* of 'solar' or spiritual importance (*potentiality*); the year's cycle is that in the planet's orbit around the Sun, in which course the planet is acting 'circonferential' or 'lunar', *i.e.* dependent as a servant on his master — so this is a cycle of dependency (*reality*) in nature. In both cases, however, Mars indicates the higher culmination, Saturn the lower. They are the two poles of one happening — but not likes. The day's cycle culminating at noon is still celebrated by the *muezzin* in his chant of praise to the Lord — but "*Arhans* (adepts) *are born at midnight hour*" says the *Voice of the Silence* (p. 39), this wonderful fragment from the (oriental) *Book of the Golden Precepts*. The cycle of the year had its four sidereal festivals at the four quarters, of which in our days only Christmas and Easter survive, and among Freemasons the third point is still commemorated: St. John's festival, reminding of the fact which has been described so beautifully in the legend of Tammuz-Adonis, who after enjoying and sharing the most perfect happiness in outer life with his beloved (Ishtar), was killed by the Boar (Cancer).

The first cycle contains the rythm of the individuality; the second one that of the (outer) personality in the (outer) world — both have their 'ups and downs'.

The same interchanging of the Mars- and Saturn-principles is stated by Kugler in his Ist book on the *Sternkunde und Sterndienst in Babel*: "It is certainly undeniable, that the deities NIN-IB and *Nergal* in the religious texts are hardly to be distinguished from one-another. Still it doesn't follow from this, that the names of the planets to which these gods were addicted, underwent the same change; this even appears impossible, where the names of the planets expressed their *nature*" (SSB, p. 220).

Jastrow relates, that Nergal next to Ninib-Ninurta is the protector of hunting, sports and war. Between him and Ninib there is hardly any difference. Like the latter he is the perfect ruler of battle who, together with Ashur, precedes the monarch. He is imagined bearing mighty weapons, which he has bestowed on the king (RBA, p. 229). Further more Weidner states the fact in his treatise on *Astronomy*.

Jastrow emphatically points out the very striking difference between Nergal-Saturn and Ea, god of the waters. The full form of the name appears to have been Ner-unu-gal. The three components of this name mean 'the mighty one of the great habitation' (RBA, p. 64).

From the latter quotation one should conclude: this confirms remarkably well the description given by classic astrologers of Saturn as the 'planet of the cristalline sphere', which was supposed to denote the limitation of our solar system proper — a supposition which is not invalidated by the finds of modern astronomy, because the latter teach a fundamental difference between the planets of the system up to Saturn and the other ones outside, whose satellites have shewn a reverse motion, a probable sequence of a reverse axial motion of the planets themselves (Uranus and Neptune; of Pluto no satellite is known as yet). In Blavatsky's *Secret Doctrine*, this sphere of Saturn is indicated as 'the ring pass not' (I, p. 63, 154, 155).

In babylonian teachings Saturn has been called 'the star of Shamash'. If — as we pleaded before — there is a certain explanation acceptable for an interchange or assimilation of Ishtar with the abstract elements (atmosphere) of the Earth and Ishtar is to become on the other hand a name for the species 'star', the said formula "Nergal is the star of Shamash" might mean: the material incarnation, bodily vehicle, or something of the kind. Then again we come on the topic of angel-demon, or god-satan. Which however is too far reaching to be worked out at present.

The 'great habitation' clearly denotes the dominion on or over which Nergal rules. He is further called the god of the kingdom of death, an other expression for the underworld. What we call the kingdom of death is a relativity: sometimes it is imagined below this world where the dead go to, descending as in a sort of pit (Hades) — compare Dante's Hell — another time we may just mean this physical world itself in which our so-called life is carried on, but which stands in flagrant opposition to that other world of dreams, which is judged to be so much more alive than this 'life' down here; at least by a good many mystics and theosophists. Anyhow Saturn is the phase of consciousness of the deepest immersion of the spirit in matter, symbolised by the lower culmination of the Sun in its apparent year's cycle around the Earth. Thus Saturn came to be called 'lord of the physical body' — immersed spirit, etc. etc. This, of course, is modern astrology, by no means Babylonian history.

Jastrow shews Nergal, surrounded by a host of lower demons, as the babylonian Pluto — this appears to make things still more intricate. In my book EEA Pluto is supposed to be related to Mars and the zodiacal sign Aries, but surely analogous with Osiris as 'lord of the underworld', judge of the death; and I have tried to prove that his standpoint must be seen as the top of the physical world, essence of this physical and bodily existence, just like the proton has to be considered as the essence and being of the physical atom. Saturn, on the contrary, is he lord of the ready formation or bodily existence, which has sprung forth from the essence. He is, after the doctrine of old as well as according to modern astrology the Former and Reaper; Pluto is the 'Initiator'. A certain analogy exists between the polarities Pluto(Mars)-Saturn, like between Sun-Moon.

The activities of Nergal-Saturn, adds Jastrow, are not limited to the rulership over death, but are found also in the embodiment of several evils, which bring death to mankind. Chiefly sickness and war. Therefore one of the most habitual ideograms for his name is that which means 'sword'. Let this again not lead to an erroneous conclusion as if Nergal would still be Mars (♂). It is well known that throughout the ages the symbol used for Saturn has been the scythe or the sickle (♄) and the sword is a thing that has always been closely related with them.

Different from Ninib (Ninurta), who was a war god as well, Nergal symbolises in particular the destruction that goes together with war, not the vehement warrior who is near his subjects in battle. Nergal is essentially the destroyer.

The latter is in accord with the astrological tradition, ancient and modern: Saturn breaks and breaks up, if he does not build or build up.

Jastrow continues: He is eventually a 'god of fire', a 'raging king', the violent one 'who burns up' and finally he is identical with the scorching heat of the flame (RBA, p. 65).

The latter is confirmed by present day Physics, which teaches: condensation sets heat free. Condensation is the saturnian principle. As such Saturn is 'lord of the fire'. As the glowing flame Nergal apparently is a phenomenon of the Sun. The Babylonians have distinguished between the successive activities and phases of the Sun; Nergal is also named as that of the blazing Sun of Midsummer and noon, the chief characteristic as such being its destructive force with regard to the local climate. This is easy to grasp. Even so if Nergal is called above all "therefore lord ot death". — Anyhow Nergal only represents a form of appearance of the solar deity. The god who is worpshipped as embodied in the Sun *par excellence,* as that Sun itself, was Shamash (RBA, p. 66). The difference is clear.

NINURTA-MARS

Ninurta-Mars is the hero among the gods (formerly the name was read Ninib) and in Nippur was considered to be the son of Enlil.

"In one prayer he was praised as 'the first among the gods', as hero and Saviour, who succoured the weak who took the body from the underworld..." — certainly a strong expression for healing of the sick — etc. etc. (HAOG, p. 377).

'Saviour' reminds of Christ, who said "Think not that I am come to send peace on earth; I came not to send peace, but a sword" (St. Matthew X 34, ed. 1841).

It is curious to see how well this expression agrees with those of a sumerian prayer, which may be dated perhaps 3000 years earlier. Without pretending to explain everything, I should like to state the conformity with the original definition as the 'star of Shamash'. It could even be said to explain a good deal of it.

'Hero' of course helds an allusion to the principle of energy, consequently to the struggle (for existence) resulting from it. For an eastern view on the necessity of the struggle for existence I beg to point to the *Bhagawad Gitâ* (first and second discourse) where this appears to belong to the teachings of Shri Krishna and to make out an important part of them.

In a series of texts, bearing an epic character, treating of Ninurta and praising him as the hero among the gods, there is this expression: like Anu thou art formed. As Heros the saga of mysterious birth is addicted to him: 'he is the son of an unknown father, he had no foster-mother and disdained the milk'. Animals, plants, stones were ruled by him in their conditions of existence. In one of the texts the plants elect the merciful Ninurta from a mountain spreading the seed, as their king (HAOG, p. 337).

Is there an analogy between Ninurta as the animal-king ruling the world of plants and minerals, and man ruling the animal, plant and mineral kingdoms all three together? (*Genesis,* I, 28, 29).

We have seen that the wife of Ninurta is called Gula, 'who renders life to the dead by touching them with her pure hand' — Gula being another name for Venus-Ishtar. We find further that his emblem is the double lion (HAOG, p. 378): during the whole of christian Middle-Ages the two lions — a red one and a white one — were the symbols of passion, the crude or carnal and the refined or sublimated.

As reported by Weidner (from starlist K. 250) Mars is also called the 'fox-star',

'star of brigands' [1]), the 'wine-red' or the 'dark-red' one, the 'rebellious', the 'hostile', the 'incalculable one'; (HBA, p. 11) while Saturn is called 'black', Mars is the 'wine-red star' and connected with Tammuz and the boar, the midsuumer-myth relating to the Ninurta-phase in the epic of the year.

In another place Weidner has (starlist II Rawl. 49) that Nebo-Mercury could be indicated as the 'star of the spotted fox'. It is difficult to make out whether here is an interchanging of Ninurta-Mars with Nebo-Mercury and if so what the meaning may be. Apparently there exists a certain relationship between both to have been intended in babylonian mythology, which we find conformed (starlist Br. M. 86378) where Mercury is identified with *ilu*Mash. "The god Mash is a form of appearance of Ninib, which in different places suggests the assimilation Ninib-Mercury..." True this is followed by: "The principal god, revealed in the planet Mercury, is Nebo, god of the West- or autumnal point...", but again: "Both these gods, Nebo and Mash, are similar in their astral characters..."; once more:... "Mercury whose name is Ninib..." (HBA, p. 42). May we venture an explanation along this line: in starlist II Rawl. 49 Mercury is also called the 'linking star', the star which lies a relation or binds. Weidner annotes: "where the linking star is to be searched in the heavens remains uncertain. Perhaps it is identical with *ilu*kamû, the 'bound god' (HBA. p. 35)?" — after which I should like to put it this way: if Mercury actually has to be considered as the star (or principle) attaching bonds, forming links, which indeed is the existing doctrine in astrology, then the binding of one's self to an object by desire is also to be acknowledged as a problem in ethics, religion and mysticism, that cannot have been very unfamiliar to the moralising Babylonians: then though the 'binder' is not identical with the 'bound one', he stands in relation to him, as one pole to the other.

Mars and Mercury are polar opposities in a way, like Saturn and Jupiter: in pairs they are called 'twin planets' (starlist V R. 46) (HBA, p. 54).

Mentioned by Jastrow we find the names Nin-gir-su (RBA, p. 86), Nin-shakh or Nin-shubur for this 'well-known god of war'; *shakh* meaning wild boar, this is the god of the wild boar. And — adds Jastrow — like sometimes Nergal is symbolised by the lion (?) the animal could be symbolising the grimly destructive nature of the godhead (RBA, p. 87).

'Servant of Anu' is this martial figure and "as such he carries the name Pap-Sukal, *i. e.* 'divine messenger'". Looks like Mercury!

Finally — says Jastrow — the names Nin-girsu, Ningish-zida and Nin-shakh are only surnames of the warlord *per excellence*, Nin-ib = Ninurta — originally solar god (RBA, p. 88).

Ungnad mentions the expression: Ninurta launched the cyclone. He also speaks of 'Ninurta's net', says that he goes to war and brings the name 'old sumerian war-god'. The principal figure of the assyrian pantheon, Ashur, is said to combat Tiamat the spirit of chaos with his monsters, and in battle he is 'armed with the cyclone' (RBAU, p. 11—13). This makes Ashur more or less identical with Ninurta-Mars. One would conclude the same from the assyrian people's very warlike nature.

Ashur may have been originally, as is supposed, a local deity in the city of that name, still he appears also as the solar god and is held in high esteem by Sargon II, when the assyrian kingdom reaches a summit of power: he is named by that king 'ruler of all the gods', 'father of the gods', 'great rock' and so on. It is Ashur who grants crowns and scepters, the kings of Assyria are only his *patesis*, his stadholders (Jastrow, RBA, p. 214). He apparently bears even a character of Sun-Saturn combined. Given the mentality of babylonian mythology, where the *four* planets all four bear solar dignity and -character, it is of course always possible to worship and put one of the four in the foreground as the special representation of the solar god.

All acts of war are carried on in the name of Ashur — Victory belongs in the first place to Ashur — ... in his service are the kings... (RBA, p. 212). Now we can wonder perhaps how and why it is said that Ishtar as well commands in battle and favours the warrior, but this is finally no more strange than stating that this

---

[1]) Saturn is also called 'brigand-star': *il*Habbatum (II Rawl. 49).

power, which conveys ordening and welfare in general, does the same to warriors as to other people. And when man feels himself above all a 'warrior' he praises Ishtar on account of favouring war, his special occupation: it means tactics; and a strategically well conducted army in battle has more success than one without the favour of 'order', tactics, strategy. Great tacticians like Wallenstein, Nelson, Napoleon, Foch underwent all of them much the influence of the zodiacal sign Libra, of venusian and ordening quality.

Jastrow says — apart from the habitual babylonian pantheon in Assyria stands only Ashur (RBA, p. 202), still his position looks very much martial in character. Owing to the strong light under which he is placed, his significance grows apparently. Ashur is symbolised by a pennant, which can be carried from one place to another, planted in the midst of the turmoil of war in order to assure to the army the presence of the god; the other gods in Assyria are represented by columns. The standard or pennant consisted of a disc flanked by two wings; the disc surmounted by the torso of a warrior shooting a shaft (RBA, p. 206).

This symbol for Ashur is wellknown and reminds of the Egyptian 'winged globe', symbol for a very high spiritual power, a power of the highest sublimation and devoted above all the powers of heaven and earth, and evidently much more 'heavenly' than the other gods who were depicted as columns of (a very) earthy material. This leaves apart the power of Ishtar, who rules at his side or next to him. The two principal residences of the assyrian kingdom bore the names of the two gods: Ashur and Nineveh.

The winged disc is so common as a symbol of the Sun in religious systems of different peoples of old, that it is hard to escape from the conviction, that it is the same in this case (RBA, p. 206). He denies, however, that the said figure means Ashur and says, that it symbolises the Sun. I cannot accept this as a pertinent denial, considering the generally accepted fact of the 'solar character' of all *four* — Ashur in Assyria as well as Marduk in Babylon. As to the name there appears to exist little certainty; Jastrow judges it probable that Ashur is a by-name of Ashir, about in the sence of 'overseer' or 'researcher', just like Marduk is named Ashir-ilâni, 'overseer of the gods (RBA, p. 207).

For Ninib-Ninurta we find also the name Lugal-Banda, which means 'strong king'. Nevertheless — this interchange again — this name has also been used for Nergal RBA, I p. 89, 172, 229).

MARDUK-JUPITER

Marduk-Jupiter who personifies the force and character of the Sun in its rising, has been called the 'saviour' and means actually the conveying of welfare, salvation, prosperity, joy and the force that illumines or sublimates as it is called in a psychological sense. If it be preposterous to convey the principle and the qualities of Marduk to the Teacher who founded the christian religion and was said to have been crucified between the two evil-doers (Mars and Saturn) about the time of the vernal equinox the Golgotha-drama nevertheless appears an image of cosmic happenings (Compare EEA, p. 63, 66).

♂ midsummer
|
|
—— ♃ spring
|
|
♄ midwinter

Here is clearly a symbolism sprung from cosmic sources at the root of the syncretistic view of life, which is the ground of mesopotamian culture.

Just like "Tiâmat was seen in the Moon, Marduk was addicted to the Sun" (HAOG, p. 168). We know in astrology that Jupiter, which is the planetary ruler of the zodiacal sign Sagittarius, is said to have its 'exaltation' in the sign Cancer, sign ruled by the Moon, and of 'chaos' — Tiâmat. The function, which was entrusted to Marduk-Jupiter, according to the epics, by Anshar, an abstract and patriarchal power in heaven shewing much analogy with Chronos-Saturn (HAOG, p. 120 and Jastrow RBA, p. 13—15), consisted in defeating Tiâmat and his monsters and the creation of definite worlds and creatures. Composing this commission with the significance which Marduk-Jupiter carries as the solar force in elevation, force of the spirit, then the said function appears as the conquest of the power of spirit on the resistance of matter or the 'underworld' — and this is the contents of Anshar's mandate.

On his merit *in casu* Marduk is promoted to 'great god', head of the lower gods [1]). Among these lower gods are counted also those 'spirits', whom we should call rather co-regents, builders, etc. (compare Blavatsky's *Secret Doctrine*), the Igigi and Anunnaki, spirits of higher and lower regions respectively. The former might be compared with the mental forces, of which Plato speaks and whom he calls 'motives' or motoric forces, *theoi*; the latter are called 'gods of the underworld', who are the guardians of the water of life and judges over the dead (Landsberger, idem Jastrow). In particular Ashur is said to be the head of the Igigi, Ishtar to wield power over the Anunnaki (Jastrow, RBA, p. 216), which reminds of the resemblance which Ashur bears to Marduk, in a certain respect, both being phases of the solar being. The astrologer puts himself also the question, whether Ashur-Mars in this case does figurate above all as the male force in nature and in heaven, ruler of the mental gods or the spirits of the element 'air', while Ishtar thus represents the female force ruling those gods of the world of feeling, *i. e.* the element 'water'.

The later Greek picturing of Zeus on the top of the Olympos ruling the world from thence as upper-god renders the comparison Marduk-Zeus indeed very plausible.

Marduk is the son of Ea — the relation of both to the zodiacal sign Pisces (Sagittarius) well known in astrology, gives a key to the said genealogical relation.

Babylon has known — finally — a sort of 'government church', in which Marduk was put at the head as *summus deus*, about 1900 b.C. under the reign of Hammurabi. In this Marduk are then united the divine legend of Enlil of Nippur together with that of Marduk, son of Ea, from Eridu; in general all mythical traits that appeared apt to make him appoint as the lord of the world and therefore of Babylon, capital of the world (HAOG p. 373).

He has always kept the quality of 'solar child'. As the national god of Babylon he is the lord of heaven and earth. Priestly documents confirm the babylonian saying in the epic of creation, that he is praised as the conqueror of the dragon, who created this world (*i.e.* Marduk) and received the dignity of Anu in reward. — 'dignity of Anu' means literally: *first class (a)*. — The babylonian priests expected 'his lordliness to be preached unto far-off peoples'. — An expectation which was repeated in Jerusalem, later: "Go and preach the gospel to all peoples of the earth." Jupiter is known in astrology as the preacher, categorical principle of spreading, radiation, emanation, expansion, *i.e.* also preaching, indeed. [2]) As such we might even assimilate Marduk with Prajapâti (Brahmâ) who in the *Bhagavad Gitâ* (III, 10) is called 'lord of emanation'.

As national god of Babylon he remained the 'lord of fate' as well, which is proved by evidences from Assyria, (starlist V R. 46), bearer of wisdom in the pantheon and the merciful one who loves awake the dead (HAOG, p. 373).

If Nergal-Saturn is lord of the kingdom of the dead, then Marduk-Jupiter, his polar opposite, must represent the force that awakes death indeed: compare the year's cycle and the function of both in it. Modern astrology still sees it in the same way and is able to prove it to a certain extent (EEA); compare also the gospel of St. John, V 21.

Marduk-Jupiter is called the 'lord of heaven and earth' *(b)* in which definition

---

[1]) An extensive treatise on Marduk is to be found in Böhl's: *Nieuwjaarsfeest en Koningsdag in Babel en Israël.*

[2]) Compare *Theosophic Glossary* by Blavatsky *s.v.*

we must certainly read the relation of the earth and heaven or, conversely, that which heaven has to offer to the earth.

In a hymn *a* and *b* are united as follows:

"Marduk, great lord, first one in heaven and earth, omniscient, cognising everything,
"Merciful god, who hears prayers and accepteth supplications,
"The light of the parts of the world, shepherd of men, art thou.
"Without thou heaven nor earth would have been created" (HAOG, p. 374).

NEBO-MERCURY

The relation between heaven and earth is laid by Marduk together with his twin-principle Nabû or Nebo. How this 'twin'-nature has to be understood, may become more or less clear from the documents in which Nabu is also called 'bearer of the decrees of fate — documents of the gods' — the 'generator of the gods'. the 'rejuvenator of the gods', the 'allwise'. These are qualities which are granted by Marduk-Jupiter, who repeatedly takes action instead of his father and who reveals the works or qualities of his father, that is why he was called the 'proclaimer' or 'preacher', the 'prophet'. The latter significance has been presented in arabic till the present day.

Direct proof exists as to the double phases (of Mercury) in assyrian omina: Mercury is 'star of sunrise' and 'star of sunset'. The mythological name of Mercury is Nabû, which means proclaimer, *i.e.* of the dawn of a new era (HAOG, p. 175).

As to the autumn-point — site or rôle of Nebo-Mercury in the year's cyclic process, function of decline, — the same in every cyclic process, Jeremias remarks: "... while to our feeling the autumnal point bears the characteristic of death, the oriental, in his dramatical-calendaric way of thinking is able to see the point of descent as a moment of coming to life, *i.e* as the passing through death to life." — with which the parallel is drawn with the christian church-year regarding the figure of St.-Michael 'conqueror of death and devil' as belonging to autumn (HAOG, p. 176).

Nabû was originally the town-god and *summus deus* of Borsippa, sister town to Babylon. The ecclesiastical doctrine of Babylon, who took this god up in the royal household of Marduk, made of him the son of Marduk and the scribe of history in the cult of Babylon.

This may be historically correct, but gives no idea about the reason why. At present, one look at the solar system, however, offers an explanation: there Mercury, placed between the Sun and Venus on one side, Jupiter placed in the same way between Mars and Saturn on the other side of the earth, are actually in polar opposite positions (compare the schemes in EEA). Babylonian documents proving the knowledge of the helio-centric system have not been found however.

The habit of promoting some or other deity to *summus deus* — *i. e.* taking some or other partial expression of the Almighty — bears no more actual meaning than taking a certain specific coloured ray instead of the central white light. In heraldism the habit was continued in Europe during many ages. The same as clans and totems being held together by some symbols and colours.

All art of writing denoting divine wisdom is wisdom of Nabû — rendered wisdom, reproduced, proclaimed, reflected, handed-over; this indeed is the function of Mercury in astrological philosophy. — His emblem, the slate pencil and tablets shew that he should be the inventor of writing. — This is a definition of the category or principle or function that *is* called Nabû or Nebo. And that is all: function of re-production etc. "His temple in Borsippa is called 'temple of the seven transmittors of commands between heaven and earth', that is: the seven planets" — which evidently means the same as we found already elsewhere, in the definition as 'the planet planet' or planet *par excellence.*

Now this reads with Jeremias literally: "In the planetary sense Nabû reveals himself, at least after the later astral doctrine, in Mercury, etc.... In the heaven of the fixed stars he is localised in the Scorpion (EN-GUN)". Now this looks like stating that the principles in themselves *are* existent, and become *localised* in some or other astronomical part or heavenly body; even so this may have been clear to the Babylonians in their theological system.

The connection of Nebo or Nabû with Marduk (also Bēl) appears from the fact that the kings send up their prayers to 'Bēl (Marduk) and Nebo', in the same way connected as 'Ashur and Ishtar'. In the time of king Adad-Nirari III Nebo becomes the "protector of the arts, as allwise who wields the pen of writers, as well as the possessor of wisdom in general..." He comes to be invoked also as the 'leader of powers', but this apparently relates more to heavenly host than to terrestrial armies (Jastrow, RBA, p. 238). The latter definitions remind of the Vulcan-Hephaistos or Vulcan-Mercury (astrologically connected with the Virgo-sphere and -sign, comp. EEA), who forged the weapons of the gods, thus putting them to arms. The other definitions are still the same as those given of Mercury today.

There is a babylonian god, a fire god, called Nusku, appearing in the conjuring texts and probably identical with Gibil or Girru — in a certain way identified with Sin and also representing one of the solar personalities — who is called by Ashurbanipal the 'bearer of the luminous sceptre', just like Nebo is named; apart from this he also appears as the wise god. The two symbols of his name, *i. e.* the sceptre and the *stylus*, are united in the person of Nusku, the same as with Nebo. Furthermore we find mentioned that this Nusku is the 'messenger of Bēl-Marduk', carrying his messages to Ea. After being the messenger of Bēl he next becomes generally the 'messenger of the gods', 'highly esteemed messenger of the gods', companion of Ashur, etc. (Jastrow, RBA, p. 232).

So this is another name for the same Mercury-Nebo principle.

XI. ANU-EA-ENLIL AS URANUS-NEPTUNE-PLUTO

The planet Uranus was vizually discovered towards the end of the 18th century, Neptune in the 19th and Pluto in the beginning of our 20th century. There can be no question about the Sumerians, nor even the later Babylonians, having observed these planets astronomically. The Greeks — says Weidner — used equinoxials, *armillae* or *astrolabia*. And "...like their whole science of the starry heavens, they will have borrowed their astronomical instruments from Babylon." Consequently such an *armilla* must have existed probably as early as 3000 b.C. — adds Weidner (HBA, p. 48). All present assyriologists, including Weidner himself, would put a later date.

Still in Greek mythology we are very distinctly informed about the qualities of the lord of the heavens, Ouranos, of the sea-god Neptune and the Lord of the underworld Pluto, who as Osiris appears as much evident in Egypt. Very often the mythological descriptions given by the Greeks are more intelligible or less enigmatical to us — their descendants in a straight line — than those of the Babylonians. Theirs are like a reproduction the drawing of which has been put up in more concise contours and therefore also more understandable to us, who strictly speaking are their disciples, because we are trained after Graeco-Roman masters. Once the faculty of observation having been awakened, however, originated in the Greek school, we are able to find easily the significances in a good many babylonian and other earlier epics and legends, theogonies. Present-day astrology guided by occidental intelligence and reason may probably and finally be of some aid to render those early epics and legends intelligible.

Now without trouble the primary divine triad Anu, Ea, Enlil is to be recognised as the triad later on presented by Greek masters, as the lords of heaven, sea and earth respectively — not as high abstractions, because the Greeks spoke no more in abstractions (only as mathesis), but nevertheless recognisable in their well defined qualities. And Ea is Poseidon as well as Enlil is the prototype for Pluto and Anu for Uranus. "As lord of the underworld Enlil is opposite to a god Anu who rules the heavenly bodies" (Jastrow, RBA p. 53). The definition dates from Hammurabi's time.

This evidently is not the Anu, abstract and highly elevated above all of early days, but a personification, as it were, participating in the regency of the concrete or created world.

About the qualities of Ea ruling the waters and 'the deep' there can be hardly any doubt. All from Sumerian times we find the name Enki for Ea and very distinct definitions as 'highest counsellor', 'god of unyielding commands' — 'from him kings receive their wisdom' —. Wellknown in modern astrology is the fact that against the influences of Neptune no human resistance or force is of any avail, only wisdom may bring help.

Rim-Sin, king of Larsa about 2250 b. C. names Ea (Enki) beside Bēl (Enlil) and calls them 'great gods'. The ideograms with which the name Enki is written, indicate him as the god of that which is below, in the first place the earth. When next the functions of the great gods are separated, he becomes the god of the waters and the deep. When this stage of speculation is reached, he is often mentioned together with Bēl, who, as we will remember, properly speaking is the 'god of the lowest sphere', but then becomes the earth-god *par excellence*. — With the Amorites, Arameans and some other groups of population the name Dagan appears in the sense of god of agriculture and earth-god, consequently identical with the babylonian Bēl (Jastrow, RBA p. 221). — So when Bēl and Ea are invoked, this is in modern parlance of the same significance as the invocation of the elements earth and water. And like Bēl in a way serves to personify the unity of the forces of earth, so Ea becomes simply the deep of the waters (RBA p. 221).

I wish to emphasize this excellent definition: Bēl-Pluto as the 'unity of the forces of the earth' — this perfectly satisfies a modern astrologer, who views Pluto, as the planetary ruler of Aries, prince or topmost power of this physical world, and will probably as well satisfy an egyptologist from the papyrus of Ani, and the *Book of the Dead*, who remembers Osiris as sitting in judgment over the deceased who leave this world on his way heavenward. Repeatedly Pluto and Neptune appear to take over from each other the title of 'lord of the underworld', but at closer investigation the meaning is different and as different as those of earth and water, though both are lying *under* the world of heaven.

Ea, the father, is the personification of knowing, Bēl that of the practical activity flowing forth from the water, like Prof. Sayce *(Hibbert Lectures*, p. 104) making use of the way of saying in Gnosticism, expresses it strikingly: only that, as indicated, Marduk takes over the rôle of the more ancient Bēl. (Jastrow, RBA, p. 63) — So this means the relation of wisdom to activity, *i.e.* soul to body (compare EEA, chpt. III).

Ea-Enki is found also under other names. There is Nin-a-gal, 'god of great strength'. This one is the protector of the art of forging. — Tubalkain?

"An other indication of Ea *e.g* is Gal-dim-zu-ab, which means 'great former of the deep'. The wife of Ea appears under the name of Nin-ki. A further and very appropriate name for this goddess is Dam-gal-nun-na, the 'great ruler of the sea'..." (Jastrow, p. 63). We do not need many more identifications of Neptune.

The question remains whether the legendary figure of Uta-napishtim — the name means: 'he who beholds the soul (life)' — who travelled the waters, the babylonian Noach, has to be considered as a personification of the god of the waters? — it is said that 'he was made the like of the gods' (Unger, *Babylon die Heilige Stadt*, p. 257 footnote).

A source from the time of the dynasty of Larsa (about 2000 b.c.) speaking of the god Asaru, the Marduk of Eridu — Jastrow also is inclined to keep him for Marduk (RBA, p. 111) — was mentioned by Böhl in *Mededeelingen uit de Leidsche Verzameling II* as very probably being identical with Osiris. Asaru in that period of sumerian culture is called 'son of Ea'. An immediate relationship between Sumer and Egypt however, has not yet been proved

Böhl's supposition gets support from astrological side, where Osiris-Asaru-Pluto can rightly be called son of Ea-Neptune indeed, astronomically, as well as Pluto moving in an orbit next to that of Neptune. Astrology would not object to a relationship between Asaru-Pluto and Ashur-Mars consequently. I did not find historical proof for it, however.

Whether in later times — and perhaps rather early even — in Babylon and Assyria principles and categorical ideas of gods are more or less mixed up and used for more or less generally accepted principles in daily life, remains a question. So we find Bēl (Enlil) assimilated to Marduk in the chief temple at Babylon. At the New-Year's festival the custom was that the King — just like at his ascent to the throne — seized the hand of the statue of Marduk — or Bēl (compare Böhl, *op. cit.* and Unger, *Babylon* p. 290). Above all Bēl-Marduk had collected in himself the qualities of the god Enlil of Nippur and therewith also conquered the serpent-dragon of the same, as te royal dignity of Babylon signified the ruling of the world. (Unger, *Babylon,* p. 209). Practically and spiritually royal dignity in Babylon ceased to exist therefore, when Xerxes had ordered the statue of Marduk-Bēl to be destroyed after a failed revolt of the Babylonians in 481 or 478 b.C. The conquest of the serpent-dragon is a symbolic picture naturally derived from the proper and original mission of Marduk, *i.e.* the conquest of Tiâmat.

The name Bēl must not trouble us further, because properly speaking it is an appellativum meaning 'the Lord'.

About the dragon itself we find what literally confirms the former: To the figure of Bēl in Babel belongs also the 'dragon at Babel', that mixed being [1]) specially devoted to the god Marduk of Babylon. It represents the ruling power of the world formerly, primeval chaos, the goddess Tiâmat, and is indicated by the Babylonians as 'the red serpent-dragon' (Mushhushshu) (*Babylon,* p. 212). — The dragon of old was the holy animal of Babylon. Before Babylon came to power and dignity, the dragon belonged to the second god of the mesopotamian-sumerian divine triad Anu, Enlil, Enki(Ea), the Enlil of Nippur, which was the central sanctuary of the Sumerians. Enlil, god of the Earth's surface, and founder of kingdoms, according to the old myth conquered the queen of original chaos, Tiâmat, the conquered one joining him. When the rulership over Mesopotamia passed to Babylon, the myth was transmitted and made to fit the new lord of the world, Marduk-Bēl. The same was done by the Assyrians, (Kap. XX) with regard to Ashur. Thus the dragon finally was adapted to the three of them: Enlil, Ashur and Bēl-Marduk. (*Babylon,* p. 213) This narrative of the struggle between Enlil (Bēl-Marduk) and Tiâmat reminds of that between Nergal and Ereshkigal. It is almost the same proceeding between the opposite poles of the male and the female.

In later times we find the same symbolical romance of Marduk-Bēl and the serpent-dragon repeated in those of Moses, St. George, Siegfried, Sir Galahad. If Marduk-Jupiter is accepted as a symbol of the elevating sublime force of spirit, and the dragon as that of the unformed chaotical and (or) destructive element of matter left to its own, if further both opponents are viewed in the psychological sense they get in human life, the whole history of the legend, repeated among so many peoples in different ages is none other than the drama of human evolution from the chaotical unto the spiritual stage where man is master over and rules the serpent-dragon in himself. A problem of spiritual evolution well worth to be honoured even with the attention of a christian era. Taking these contents of the Bēl-and-the-dragon-of-Babel-legend for granted, the comparison of Marduk-Bēl with the figure of Christ does not look blasphemous.

Unger confirms the above idea of the parallel: At the feet of the godhead a holy animal reposes, the so called 'dragon of Babel', the image of Tiâmat, whom the god has once conquered and, together with the other 'previous gods', placed among the stars in the 'heavenly ocean' (*Babylon,* p. 210).

---

[1]) In german the expression *Mischwesen* is used for the sort of creatures (beings?), who generally existed of lower elements but might become mixed with some higher elements as well. Babylonian mythology even knows *Mischwesen* that are partly human.

The conquered dragon was called 'holy' after its defeat. The problem of the previous or 'former' gods, conquered by Marduk, is a very fascinating one in itself, but we shall leave it here. We venture *one* question: is the legend of so many former (earlier?) gods conquered by Marduk and placed among the stars another point of resemblance between this elevating Marduk-Jupiter and Christ, whose followers claim exactly the same conquest for him?

The most interesting feature of the Bēl-figure are the wings which the 'former Marduk' or 'older Marduk' carried (*Babylon*, p. 221). Wings bear always relation to an exalted condition of existence or life, above earthy or 'surface'-conditions; heavenly or cosmically, abstract, universal. A universal symbol indeed.

In Assyria, at Ashur, Bēl was called by Tiglat-Pileser I, 'the elder one'. Sargon II — the archeologer among the kings of Assyria (721—705 b. C.) — calls Bēl also 'the great mountain' and 'lord of the lands'. Bēl consequently was honoured in Assyria as well. We find a tale describing him as living 'on the holy mountain' on which the gods are born (Jastrow RBA, p. 236); which confirms the identification with Zeus-Jupiter-Marduk. Whether he (Sargon) or his scribes really intended a distinction between this one (Bēl-Ashur) and Bēl-Marduk, is difficult to say (RBA, p. 236).

The question how the image of Bēl-Enlil-Asaru-Osiris-Pluto could possibly represent the 'elder Marduk' can perhaps be explained to a certain extent in EEA (two tables on pp. 30, 31). Both remind us of the later image of the 'mountain of light' among the Romans.

The expression Bēl, properly signifying 'lord' is therefore also added sometimes as prefix to the other divine personalities in cases where stress is laid on their dignity. The general nomination of '*the* Lord' can also be read from it.

The history of 'Bēl and the dragon' is too important as a spiritual monument, to pass it unnoticed. — Let us quote from Unger's *Babylon, the Holy City*:

The triumph over the monster, formed as an animal, reveals the essential nucleus of an old oriental vision of life. Man in his inner-most being was considered as good. The evil done by him or the mischief oppressing him comes to him from outside. — Man was perfect and the idea of sin and debt was perfectly strange to the founders of mesopotamian culture, the Sumerians. Only by a gradual semitic influence, active since 2800 b. C., the feeling of a personal sin of mankind was awakened and spread. The Sumerians on the contrary described their gods after the model of the good man, in great contrast to Egypt, where the world of the gods came forth from the animal cult and fetichism. As the particular polar opposite to man the animal counted in Mesopotamia. It was seen as evil and inimical to man.

So the lower gods were formed as double-creatures, half man half animal or even totally animal. The Sumerians constructed such double-creatures all from the most remote times — compare the *chimères* and *gargouilles* in mediaeval Gothic.

In Sumeria through all times a steadfast fundamental thesis can be traced of double-creatures taking a higher rank the more human elements they possess; the more animal elements they contain or if existing of animal elements exclusively, the more terrifying a demon, dangerous to mankind and spreading ruin and illness they become (*Babylon*, p. 215). Compare here Staudenmaier *op. cit.*

The conquest over the dragon therefore means a great triumph over the most desastrous being. At the same time, however, this victory means an extraordinary boon to mankind. The demoniacal opponent was destroyed and mankind liberated could praise the godhead anew (*Babylon* p. 215).

This is humanism, evidently proceeding from the Sumerians, coming in conflict with, or suppressed by, a vision of life from semitic side, which was directed more against the sinful, *i.e.* demoniacal side of man. Of course the problem is one and the same: the conquest of the animal element by the human in man; the way in which it was presented is opposite. These different visions finally give rise to the questions — Unger does not answer them — how a 'liberated man' stands towards a god whom he has to bring thankgivings continually and why he should? — In the mean time the idea of being liberated (*i.e.* saved) by the 'higher Marduk' has doubtlessly passed into Indaism and Christianity. Moses who prayed for his people, to take away the serpents from them —

after which Moses is said to have made 'a serpent of brass' evidently as a remedy and as a memorial of the dangerous monster (*Numbers*, XXI, 7—9). Afterwards it gave rise to a whole christian sect calling themselves after this recorded fact, 'elevators of the serpent' — Ophites. Compare Blavatsky, *The Secret Doctrine*, II, p. 220, etc. This name-giving-fact, however, makes us ask if the 'erection' of a pole upon which the brass serpent was put, meant a symbol in itself, *i.e.* a symbol for the 'elevating' of the serpent-element in man himself. — This would simply be repeating the act of the 'older Marduk'.

The saying: Anu is the king of the Igigi and Anunnaki, *i. e.* of all the heavenly and earthy spirits, in his quality of the highest one and god of the heavens (Jastrow, RBA, p. 218), certainly does not allude to Anu in his highest abstract being, but in his function of god of the heavenly regions in a more direct and concrete sense, like Uranus. That means, however: higher than the god of the *visible* Sun. As such he is above Ashur and Ishtar as well, who come to appear as second in command to him. He is connected to physical creation as they are. In a way Anu is assimilated here with Marduk, or the reverse; which also confirms the former's relation with the concrete world. In the sense of the Gnosis therefore Anu, Enlil, Ea are relatively lower divine beings, with regard to the fundamentals of things (HAOG, p. 348, comp. 326).

Evidently Anu makes his appearance in this created world just like Bēl and Ea after all, then they all stand in relation with the motives that animate this world, each has a departement of it under his regency. Very clearly we find now-a-days the same qualities in modern astrology addicted to these planets outside the orbit of Saturn and experimentally found to hold good! Uranus was recognised by modern astrology as god of the heavens and the fact is that he displays qualities which were ascribed formerly to Anu. Neptune practically shows the qualities addicted to Ea-Poseidon-Neptune (and Varuna in India), while Pluto since its discovery in 1930 has offered but very little opportunity for experimentalising as yet, so much so that with regard to practical astrology we must leave it out of account. In EEA — first edition of 1912 in the Netherlands — the qualities were predicted along the way of deduction and these are covering those of Enlil Bēl-Pluto-Osiris of the ancient theogonies (compare EEA, 1931 engl. ed.).

This statement only means to emphasize how much Babylonian cosmogony had already found out and well defined human principles of activity and life, which long afterwards could be defined astrologically. With the following this premiss is to be kept in mind.

Anu — "...the god who, theoretically standing at the top of the babylonian pantheon, eventually appears in the inscriptions from the time of Hammurabi" (Jastrow, RBA, p. 84).

According to the regulation of the babylonian calendar it was in the 11th month of the year that a festival was celebrated in honour of Anu — ... god of the heaven *par excellence* ... Now Uranus, whom modern astrology calls the god of the heaven is the planet to whom it ascribes rulership over the *eleventh* zodiacal sign, Aquarius.

This Anu was not much in favour originally — which can very well be explained by the following annotation by Jastrow: "... a god of the heavens is an abstract idea" — very true and sufficient an explanation for the lack of popularity, with a good many among the priests even, let alone with profane circles. Uranus in modern astrology is one of the planets ruling the etheric regions.

In the mythical texts he appears as a peevish god, turning his back to the world and little inclined to men (HAOG, p. 348).

As his riding animal is named the Mushhushshu, afterwards allotted to Marduk.

In the Gilgamesh epic — (HAOG, p. 349) — Ishtar appears as the daughter of Anu and as well as his wife — the representation dates from sumerian-accadian times.

XII. THE ZODIAC

The human element is the higher, the conquering, the good. The animal is the subordinate and evil element — says Unger (*Babylon die Heilige Stadt*) on the question treated above.

In a relief sculptured in the rocks near Maltaja under the reign of king Sanherib of Assyria (about 700 b. C.) seven (planetary?) gods are represented as mounted on their riding animals (dragon, lion, bull, horse, etc.) not realistically but standing erect upon the backs of the animals. This appears to me as an illustration of the sentence quoted before, *i.e.* as a specimen of the inherent humanistic faith of the Babylonians.

Relief of Maltaja.

In modern astrology very distinctly and clearly the relation between planetary powers and zodiacal categories is viewed as of positive, active, masculine or electric forces towards negative, passive, feminine or magnetic categorical principles (compare my N. Ph. and EEA). It is on this ground that the zodiac of constellations has been called the 'heavenly Earth'. This fundamental idea has also been expressed in the relief of Maltaja evidently. In the whole of babylonian cosmogony we find the Sun, Moon and planets as the dwelling places (or embodiments) of certain gods, but at the same time as indicating certain collective hierarchies of gods, who are masculine beings generally. Next we find spoken of stargroups or constellations and of sole fixed stars as possessing a certain congeniality with planetary principles (as rulers), but in how far such asterisms are to be considered as gods, is an open question: we often do find the prefix *il* used (*e.g.* *il*Apin: Cassiopeia), and *il* or *ilu* means 'god'. The asterism of the Scorpion is said to have some relationship with Mercury. For the rest this need not appear stranger than the conclusion of modern astronomy addicting to the Pleiades, or rather to its central star Alcyone, the rôle of centre of our galactic system, which leads to a certain analogy between this central star and the centre of our solar system. The other analogies (Mercury with the Scorpion, Venus with the Hyades, eventually also with the Pleiades, Cassiopeia and Sagittarius with Mars etc.) are not to be proved presently, as far as I see. The only thing that we can trace is that after the fall of the gods in incarnations as human personalities, the 'former gods', conquered by Marduk, reappearad in the 'heavenly Earth' among the stars under animal names of different nature (*Babylon*, p. 215). These 'former gods' were thus replaced as 'stars' in the heavens — becoming or remaining masculine, active entities seemingly. But the evidence is that they were charged with the duty of representing the 'heavenly Earth', which means astrologically that these powers were compelled to build the earthy bodies, *i.e.* to furnish the lower earthy elements, the negative, passive, feminine or magnetic part in human existence down here. Which is quite what modern astrology thinks of them and proves them to be. The maxim behind this is: like only knows like, and only the relatively feminine 'earthy' or zodiacal element in heaven *could* furnish the feminine 'earthy' or bodily on earth.

The zodiacal belt (of constellations) is the 'heavenly Earth' — and because Enlil is considered to be 'lord of the earth', the pole of the ecliptic, which means the middle of the animal belt, was named 'Enlil-point'. In the same way the pole of the equator (North-pole) is the Anu-point, as Weidner (HBA, p. 33) annotates on starlist II Rawl. 49,3. This is a very important remark, because from it follows the law for so-called secundary (or astronomical) progression in astrology: *'a day for a year'* (compare *Ezekiel* IV, 6: "I have appointed thee each day for a year"). It is the equity of the daily cycle of the Earth around its axis with the course of the Earth in its orbit in the annual cycle.

What, however, is the function and the origin of the zodiac precisely? Never the zodiacal images are to be found as representing gods properly.

The babylonian names for the zodiac as *Harrân* *ilShamash*, 'way of the Sun' and also *Harrân* *ilSin*, 'way of the Moon', point to a secondary rôle and moreover to the idea of the cycle: the year's and also the month's cycle. Jeremias says about this: It is very likely that in older times the ecliptic was not particularly kept apart from the belt of asterisms (HAOG, p. 201).

In relation to the annual seasons, astronomy speaks of 'the point Aries — Cancer — Libra — Capricorn'. These are the so-called cardinal points of the ecliptic cycle. Astronomy here uses the same names as astrology. Now if we divide this circle into 12 even parts, starting from the cardinal points or corners, we get the division of the ecliptic, which by modern astrology is called the 'zodiac of the Earth' and which bears the significance of cycle between the Sun and the Earth during a year and depicted in the 'aura' of the Earth as the astrological saying is. Parts of 30 degrees of arc each. The twelve star-groups at the firmament, which from old form the 'heavenly belt' of 'animal-signs' contain stars placed on very much different distances from the Earth. They are moreover not exactly limited to 30 degrees. In ancient astrology they were considered as 'the twelve houses of the gods', lying at a dwelling street or dam. Therefrom came the nomination 'heavenly dam' for the zodiacal belt of asterisms, and also 'enclosure of heaven' (HAOG, p. 139). The descriptions apparently include the fact that they were invented and given by people living in low countries on the banks of a river, which from time to time flooded the land and where, consequently, a dam was needed to build the houses upon. In the same way the houses of the gods were imagined as being built upon a dam cast up against the heavenly ocean (HAOG, p. 139). The latter could be considered a symbolical saying — the Babylonians and Sumerians thinking much in symbols — and this might have meant that the gods in this material world had to accept or to choose a dwelling-place (a body) of material nature, the latter being a physical precipitate or condensation. An idea very common in mysticism, occidental as well as oriental.

The heavenly bodies of our solar system are walking along the way of this heavenly dam — thus was the idea.

A particular comparison made by the Babylonians was that between the zodiac and the rainbow. "Zodiacal belt and rainbow belong together mythologically" — confirms Weidner (HBA, p. 14). (Compare the coloured print in EEA).

The seven planets — treading the way of the zodiac — which properly is a rainbow of the seven colours — does it not look like the sevenfold rythm in chemistry as well as in music — *n'en déplaise* the finds of so many new chemical elements in the later years?

As soon as seven planets were counted (and there was never a time to be imagined when this was not done) the seven colours were ascribed to them, a parallel with the seven-coloured rainbow lying ready at hand (HAOG, p. 139).

Considering the generally accepted idea of the great importance of cycles, a natural sequence is to devote attention to the year as well as to the day and to the star-groups which have to do with the precessional cycle. The Babylonians did. Still with the plastic way of thinking, proper to the Mesopotamians, this has not been spoken out literally in a philosophical way, as far as I know.

Jeremias puts the question, in what time the circle of phantastic images, which we call the 'animal belt', has been invented, consequently at what time it became to be considered as stations on the way of the Moon, the Sun, Jupiter, etc. ('houses'), and in particular in what time the street became divided into 'zodiacal signs' of 30 degrees each, paying no attention to the different lengths of the zodiacal groups, but founding the division on the twelvefold. It became necessary as soon as the heavens, after having been no more than a picture book in the ancient gnostic way of viewing, also became a book of arithmetics (HAOG, p. 202).

Up to the present time literature procures no text older than 420—419 b. C. in which the twelve constellations are related (Meissner BA, II, p. 406).

A propos of 'lunar stations' — we know that the Hindus counted 27 or 28 lunar stations — with the Babylonians there are 24. Moon's orb and zodiac have been brought on accord already: the 24 lunar stations agree with the 12 zodiacal signs — is Weidner's annotation on star-list Br. M. 86378 (HBA, p. 51).

Anyhow, the 'zodiacal signs', well known to everybody from the calendar, partially reminding of Egyptian hieroglyphs, are very ancient.

"The babylonian origin of the zodiac hardly finds contradiction any more. The question remains how it was divided in the remotest times and how it became to be gradually pictured as that which we now use to call the zodiac with its twelve signs" (HAOG, p. 202).

About the origin of the zodiac I decline suggestions and I emphatically refuse every sort of belief to assurances of it having been 'invented' by some one at some time or other. There has been known a zodiac in ancient Peru before the reign of the Inca-dynasty as has been duly reported by Garcilazo de la Vega; there are as well reports about a chinese zodiac — or rather two — and both appear to be able to boast an antiquity of about 13000 years b. C. as I have tried to prove elsewhere. So this does not encourage supositions about some 'inventor' or some year of invention, nay even not about a special period of culture which could have produced it.

The names for the zodiacal signs gathered from different sources are given here:

	Thompson (*Reports*, p. XXIII—XXIV) and Kugler SSB, I, 1907, p. 30		*Jastrow* (RBA, p. 679—684)	*Jeremias* (HAOG, p. 210—213) (From the *Te*-table)	
	late babylonian	assyrian		500 b. C.	566—565 b. C.
♈	Ku(sarikku)	Enmesara	Ku-Mal	Ku-Mal	Ku-Mal = (Hun-Gâ)
♉	Te-te	Gud-Anna	Gu-An-na	Mul-Mul (Zappu)	Gu-An(-Na)
♊	Tuâmu	Tuâmu	Mash-Tab-ba (tu-âmê)	(Mash-Mash)	Mas-Tab(-Gal) Mas-Tab(-Tur)
♋	Pulukku	Al-lul	Al-lul [1]	Al-lul	Star Presepe = the cot
♌	Arû	Urgula, Urmah	Ur-Gu-La (Ur-Makh)	Ur-Gu-La	Ur-A
♍	Shiru	Shiru	Ab-Shin (= Esh-shin)	Ab-Shin (= Esh-shin)	Eshshin
♎	Zibanitu	Zibanitu	Zibanitu	Zibanitu	Zibanitu
♏	Akrabu	Akrabu	Gir-Tab (Akrabu)	Gir-Tab	(Antares = Ne-Gun)
♐	Pa	Pabilsag	Pa-Bil-Sag	Pa-Bil-Sag	Pa-Bil
	Enzu	——	Sukh-khur-Mash (Kha)	Suḫur	Suḫur-Mash
♒	Gu	Gu-Anna (?)	——	Gula	——
♓	Nunu	Nun-Shamê	Kha-Fish	—— [2]	Shin-Maḫ

For the names of the zodiacal signs Kugler gives the following list on the authority of text Rm. 105, by Pinches (Academy 4 November 1893) and Virolleaud:

---

[1]) Akkadian: Nangaru.

[2]) Weidner gives: Zibbāti ('the tails').

1.	*Nisannu*	KU. MAL	Aries
2.	*Airu*	MUL. MUL + GÙ. AN. NA	Pleiades + Taurus
3.	*Sivanu*	SIB. ZI. AN. NA. MAS. TAB. BA. GAL. GAL. A	Orion + Gemini
4.	*Dūzu*	AL. LUL	Cancer
5.	*Abu*	UR. GU. LA	Leo
6.	*Ulūlu*	AB. SIM	Virgo
7.	*Tišritu*	*Zi-ba-(ni-tu)*	Libra
8.	*Araḫ-samna*	GIR. TAB	Scorpio
9.	*Kislimu*	PA. BIL. SAG	Sagittarius
10.	*Ṭebitu*	SUḪUR	Capricorn
11.	*Šabatu*	GU. LA	Aquarius
12.	*Addaru*	DIL. GAN [1]) + *rikis nūni*	DIL. GAN + Link of the Fishes.

(*Ergänzungen*, Part II, 1914, p. 168)

A definite teaching on the categorical significance of each of the twelve signs in the zodiacal cycle is not known. Perhaps it has not been realised in detail; it may have been kept a secret or not been put into writing. The oriental gnosis — says Jeremias — with Jews and other peoples, speculating upon the divine regents of the four corners of the world as the commanders of angelic hosts was in the line of ancient oriental piety, which coupled the idea of the activities of certain divine forces of manifesting at certain points, with phenomena in the cosmos in terms of the cycle (HAOG, p. 213).

In the library of Ashurbanipal a list has been found containing the names of the twelve angels of the months. With the gradual acceptance of the zodiac as the twelvefold circle, which was then divided into regular parts of 30^0 as a zodiacal sign each, the month's angels became zodiacal angels. (HAOG, p. 214) Therefrom the custom to apply the twelve zodiacal categories to daily life on Earth has been derived: — the 'twelve tribes of Israel', which are said to agree with the twelve mansions of the zodiac; the twelve towns of the Etrusks, the twelve tribes of the Arab and Ishmaëlites, and of the Perses; the twelve countries addicted to the zodiacal signs, etc.

Actually we ought to acknowledge that we know as good as nothing about this matter in Mesopotamian culture. There are indications of something existing, but nothing in the way of direct teaching. The twelvefold cycle, however, appears to have been adopted in this culture gradually in its cosmological meaning, consequently ruling everything in the happenings on Earth. Maybe our habit to negociate things by the dozen, descends from it, even resisting the introduction of the decimal system.

Notwithstanding the lack of proper items on the point, Jeremias has gathered some stray astrological indications about each of the twelve images — by the Babylonians they were actually regarded as images in the heavens — and we will quote the sparse but interesting material:

ARIES. Very often parts of Cetus and the Fishes are collected together with this sign so that it appears more or less as a transittory phase. The only distinct description seems to be that as *agricultural labourer*. Nebukadnezar calls himself the 'agricultural workman of Babylon'. This is in the time when the vernal equinox stood in the Ram (asterism); about 600 b.C. "... the Ram opens the month-star-symbolism of the Gilgamesh epic; with the Ram opens also the month-starlist of Boghaz-Köi handed down from about 1350." This is Aries-period.

TAURUS. The Babylonians viewed the image as a bull attached to a chariot. One would say: it is the sign Taurus considered from the practical side and in daily life. Dating from the time when the vernal equinox passed through the asterism of the Bull is the idea of the heavenly bull let loose on the request of Ishtar to

---

[1]) This is corroborated by the evident relation of the constellation DIL-GAN, which covers the Pisces Australis and part of the constellation Aries, and was called "the house of Ea, predecessor of the constellation of *Anu*" — the latter of course meaning Aries (Kugler, *Ergänzungen* IInd Part, 1914, p. 167).

fight Gilgamesh. Remarkable is the fact that we repeatedly meet indications having to do with the great precessional cycle, divisions in the great course of evolution of mankind, far above the year's and the month's cycles. The significance of the image of the Bull as that of the first lunar station is taken by Jeremias as relating to the precessional period of the Bull only. The pretention that it survived the said period harbouring no special meaning, however, in it self, does not appear to be proved. (HAOG, p. 215/16). Jeremias himself quotes that the Hindus also consider the Pleiades (Kṛttika) as the first lunar station, and the Chinese in the time of the Han-dynasty Aldebaran as the first night-station of the month (Sin). It looks rather difficult to ascribe a similar nomenclature with so different peoples to one special periodical phenomenon only. The reason is not mentioned in the documents. Astrologers of the present are acquainted with the special relationship existing between the Moon and the zodiacal sign Taurus, which they say is his 'exaltation' and in which sign may be seen the strongest objectivity of the lunar principle. This is difficult to explain, however.

GEMINI. It was seen as two male twins. There was a tale of 'the great twins' being the northern, evidently Castor and Pollux, and on the other side, the southern stars ot this asterism, which are standing near Orion. Gnostic-mythologically they count as manifestations of Nabu (PA) and Marduk (LUGAL), *i.e.* as divine brothers who, later in the Greek saga, we named Castor and Polyneukes. The Dioskures myth is rich in motives which procured material for the studying of the legend.

CANCER. The sumerian word Allul (akkadian: Tittu) probably means lobster, cancer. An interesting remark is made by Jeremias: the akkadian word for the sign, Nangaru, originally possesses the significance of the asterism Presepe: the cot — in which the legend says Christ is born: the symbolical horoscope of Christ with the Sun in the midwinterpoint at midnight shews Libra ascending and Cancer on the upper meridian. A cot gives, just like the pincers of a lobster, the semi-circular line of the crescent Moon. Böhl makes the remark, that the proper meaning of Nangaru is 'carpenter', the name for the social standing which the legend ascribes to the father of Jesus; in astrology the tenth house (midheaven or upper meridian) is said to indicate the social standing of the father. The remarkable thing consequently is this, that the legend clearly shows where it originated, *i. e.* among a semitic population. The importance of the rôle played by Cancer seems to point to an analogy between Christ-being and lunar nature. From the Boghaz-Köi starlists can also be derived the definition for Cancer as the sign of the artisan or carpenter, in connection with 'the cot' and particularly to the near star Sirius (HAOG, p. 218).

LEO. The lion is mentioned by the Babylonians as a Lioness. Regulus is viewed as the lion's heart and called 'king's star'. The Chaldeans must have seen it as the lord of the heavenly world and have brought it into relation with kings on earth (HAOG, p. 218).

VIRGO. The sumerian as well as the akkadian name for this sign means ear of corn. There is no doubt about this sign having been seen already very early as one of the revelations of the Madonna-universal-mother. Therefore we may expect the asterism to resemble the madonna with the corn-ear. At the same time, however, the other image must have been known, *i. e.* that of 'the virgin with the child' (HAOG, p. 219). Both are mentioned side by side by Teukros the Babylonian. There is also the mentioning of a 'virgin with the balance'. Evidently this has to do, however, with the following sign, Libra, and with a complicated vision, looking over to Scorpio even, as the Scorpio-card in the Tarot-system suggests: VIII, Justice (compare GBT). The principal star of the sign Virgo, Spica, appears as the Madonna-star *par excellence* (HAOG, p. 220).

LIBRA. This sign apparently is always considered as a balance. With the Babylonians it must have had to do with the idea of day- and night-'evening', day and night 'together keep the balance'. Very interesting is the fact that the bearer of the balance of the dead, which is that of the world's judgment in calendaric symbolism, was related to Saturn. To grasp the idea behind it, we must remember that in oriental thought the spring- as well as the autumnal-point count as the world's turningpoints. The latter is the point of death, but in the sense of death-and-life-mystery, which procures the new by passing through death (and judgment). With the Jews the autumnal new-year's festival therefore is the festival of the world's judgment, in Christianity the autumn-point represents St. Michael, the conquerer of death and devil, who nevertheless is Michael with the balance, judge of the world in the sense of the above symbolism (HAOG, p. 221). The 'exaltation' of Saturn is said to take place in the sign Libra, and after astrological lore it means that the form-building Saturn gets his utmost (exalted) efficiency in this sign, which denotes the unity of the two opposite poles, *i.e.* the natural form or the body in nature.

SCORPIO. The gnostic astrological views connected with Scorpio are still obscure. Two Assyrian astrological documents consider the Scorpion as the revelation of the Madonna as the 'ruler of life', apparently as a waternimph, in accordance with Annunit in the northern Fish of the zodiac. — In an astrological text of an other nature Gir-Tab is called 'lord of heaven and earth'. — Its most luminous star, Antares, 'the breast of the Scorpion' in sumerian is called NEGUN [1]) or Nabû (HAOG, p. 222/23) *i.e.* Mercury. An other source of the time of Gudea mentions a weapon of a double nature to be a wand of Ninurta encircled by serpents, which seems to point to Ninurta-Ningirsu. This reminds of Mars who after the common astrological doctrine 'rules' Scorpio.

SAGITTARIUS. In an old text-book it is said that behind the Scorpion is a shooting centaur standing. Boundary stones of Nebukadnezar I shew the Sagittarian in the same way as is found on the circular zodiac of Denderah, which dates from Augustus' time. Much more has not been mentioned. The images are clearly recognisable as exemples for the later greek Centaur, our present symbol of Sagittarius. [2])

CAPRICORN. The Babylonians call this asterism a Goat-Fish and draw it in such a way as to hide the hind parts of the fish by a sort of pedestal (HAOG, p. 224) — sometimes. We know the same image of Capricorn deriving from India. It has been preserved in the same form till the present time. In the names the double significance comes to expression.

AQUARIUS. The name used by the Babylonians was *mul Gula* "the asterism of the great man". We shall easily recognise in it the zodiacal sign Aquarius, because it is still called the sign of Man. This GU. LA (the great one) must not be taken for *il*Gu-la, *i.e.* the 'goddess Gu-la', who is viewed in the Lyre and Hercules, particularly in Alpha Lyrae (Wega) as the 'ruler of life' (HAOG, p. 225).

PISCES. Great attention was paid to the 'cord (or tie?) of the fishes', which is lying between the asterisms of the northern and the southern Fish. The southern part is drawn as a fish with a swallow's head (HAOG, p. 226). Böhl asks: is perhaps the idea of 'tails' intended to mean swallow's tails? — Zibbāti.

All this renders no astrological values to boast of. If we were not acquainted — in modern astrology or astrosophy partly developed deductively — with cosmic coherence of the zodiacal signs as a system, we would be hardly able to find it from these scanty items. Neither could we reconstruct the zodiac on them. Some particulars shew that the Babylonians and already probably the Sumerians must have *known* much, if not essentially all, about the zodiac. Take for instance the relation of Saturn with Libra and of the Moon with Taurus. And this *is* important — perhaps more than eventual astronomical observations of the precessional cycle, about which there has been so much controversy.

The day was divided in twelve hours, 'double' or 'planetary' hours as they were called afterwards. 'Zodiacal hours' would have been a more apropriate name. The day's

---

[1]) *Ne. Sun* being a misprint in HAOG (p. 222).

[2]) The best reproduction reposes on a seal-cylindre in the Leiden *Rijks-Museum van Oudheden* and was collected by Prof. Böhl in 1932.

cycle became analogous with the zodiac and its twelve signs, resembling the year with its twelve months (HAOG, p. 242).

Schlegel in his *Uranographie Chinoise* has already demonstrated in 1875 that there must have been two zodiacs in China, one of which doubtlessly relates to the constellations or cosmological categories, the other being less evident, says the author, but certainly related to more earthy and 'animal' matters, a zodiac of the earthy elements. "It can be followed from Turkestan to Japan" says Jeremias, and in his turn about the same appreciation appears to be held by Edouard Chavannes in his *Cycle Turc des douze Animaux*.

The names for the signs of this lower sort of zodiac are given as (Chavannes, p. 52 rat, ox, tiger, hare, dragon, serpent, horse, goat, ape, cock, dog, swine. Compare HAOG, p. 243.

Comparing these names with those of the zodiacal signs presently in use, leads to remarkable discoveries. Putting the two lists of names side by side does not shew very marked coincidences; on the contrary: there are rather marked differences. But if we take the fifth name of this chinese animal cycle to be indentified with Scorpio, the horse falls to Sagittarius, the goat to Capricorn, the ape to Aquarius, the cock to Pisces, the dog to Aries, the swine to Taurus (ox and swine appear to have changed their places), the rat to Gemini, the ox to Cancer, the tiger to Leo, the hare to Virgo and the dragon (of wisdom?) to Libra. — Which looks remarkably well.

Now if we take the hint of the interchanging of places by ox and swine — we soon find out that there are properly speaking two zodiacs, the one speaking through the other and being sixty degrees of arc or two 'signs' apart. This is the relative condition of the zodiac of asterisms and the earthy zodiac during the Gemini-period (about 6500—4400 b. C.) — which renders a valuable item with regard to the probable antiquity of this animal-cycle.

Jeremias opening his chapter on the *Dodekaoros* says: After the sumerian way of thinking the cycle of time is as well a world of space. Together with the imagination of a twelvefold zodiac a circle of countries was bound up, which in Hellenism has been called *dodekaoros*, every country being ruled or influenced by one of the twelve signs (HAOG, p. 242/43).

The principle of every legend of creation is duality and therefore every theogony springs from duality: heaven and earth in the first place, male-female or Spirit-Matter finally. Thus it was in mesopotamian culture and creed: the maxim "as abov so below" intrinsically presupposes an 'above' and 'below'. The writer has tried to work on these principles in EEA. In the Hindu 'egg of Brahma' two kernels — one of spirit and one of matter — are the remnants and the seeds of every creation. They remind of Jupiter-Zeus-Marduk-Sun *versus* Saturn-Pan-Nergal-Moon. Perhaps the duality in the Gilgamesh epic, Gilgamesh-Enkidu is to be considered as a specimen of the same.

The gods in babylonian theogony are all represented as being accompanied by their wives, who are standing in a 'subordinate position' as Jastrow reports; the latter being like the shadows of the male gods — reflections in matter, or on the material plane; *in concreto*? *phenomena*? — are the gods, then to be viewed as *noumena*? — Was Plato right? Are the male gods to be viewed as the creative or motoric energies (belonging to the life of the soul), their spouses representing the physical 'shadows' or vehicles, as theosophy in our days again teaches? Ani in the Egyptian *Book of the Dead*, presenting himself to Horus-Mercury is accompanied by his wife. Compare *Genesis* I, 27 and II, 22; Moses and the whole of Christianity are accepting the same duality. An important and natural sequel to light is shadow. The soul is considered as an entity which, receiving the light of the spirit, throws its shadow on earth, which is called the body or embodiment. This is a mystic formula of creation.

Summa summarum — says Jeremias — this astrological vision of life has certainly not to be considered solely as that doubtful science of the Chaldees — a title far from honorific in the days of the Greek. Evidently these 'Chaldees' were poor and degenerate descendants of an illustrious past — I should like to add.

All ancient-sumerian-babylonian knowledge of the heavens was a piece of religion, nay it was the heart of religion (HAOG, p. 245).

This is satisfactory as the real base of the old sumerian-babylonian starlore: it is 'the heart of religion'.

How far later generations kept and guarded the primeval purity, is another question. As far as I see astronomy came up and astrology went to its decline when the ciphers came to take the place of the heavenly images. The 'scripture of the heavens' was probably lost, save some formulae, lost as an exalted vision of life and religion to become gradually a knowledge of horoscopy.

The historian's duty, however, is not to judge faculties of human consciousness. He is the recorder of facts. We have thought it our duty to read the significance of the recorded facts as far as possible and admissible — and to judge it after the knowledge of those who *understand* the language of the Mythos — which we do not boast of and in which we are ready to stand aside for our betters. We, modern astrologers, do *study* that language indeed and the writer of the present lines has.

APPENDIX

On the orientation of temples in Mesopotamia there have been given so different views, some of them apparently in connection with the ruling astrological vision of life, that we cannot leave this matter altogether without mentioning.

Eckhard Unger, in *Babylon, die Heilige Stadt,* did not point out many more motives for the said orientation than the winds ruling in the country. Generally it is the southwester with its very disagreeable and even dangerous gusts of wind and sand-storms from the scorched desert, which made the people of that country mindful of cover. The north-west wind was cool and refreshing, the nort-easter charged with clouds and rain. This was what constituted the directions for the groundplanes of the temples: "not the astronomical directions, however" (*Babylon,* p. 124). Scientific astronomy is often, but wrongly, supposed to have existed from the remotest times, but has not had any determining influence". — "Ciphering book was the heaven not before the 7th or 6th century (b. C.) in Nineveh and Babylon, and the monumental effect of it is the exact astronomical orientation by Nebukadnezar II of three palaces in Babylon, which lie accurately North. Then only scientific astronomy gets its influence on profane architecture. Even then it has no definite influence on sacral culture" (p. 127).

The orientation on the directions of the wind can have still another reason than one of a practical nature: excluding the hot and dusty gales from the desert. There may be found a spiritual reason for it as well — says Unger; revelation by the deity is regarded as taking place by means of the breath of wind (*Babylon,* p. 128).

The latter is perhaps less known to them who do not understand the language of the Mythos. Some Greek and Alexandrian philosophers have used the simile of the breath of man for a symbol of creation (*pneuma*) and the 'breath of God'. The name Brahma is said to derive from *brih,* breathing.

So Unger's idea about the orientation of temples in Mesopotamia apparently does not lack spiritual background. Perfectly opposed to it however is the conception of the engineer Günther Martiny in his dissertation on *Die Kultrichtung in Mesopotamien.* He accepts two principal directions of orientation: one in Babylonia on the south-west, and another in Assyria with the principal frontside north-west. Some cases remain in which south-east has been found, as in the old plan at El-Ubaid, the Ninmach- and Gula-temples at Babylon and the older Ishtar temples in Assyria, which are pointing north-east. He considers admissible the supposition that the two principal orientations must be put on account of the directions from which the peoples who built them had come. The Babylonians after 2700 b. C. came from the Arabian desert in the south-west; the people who ruled Assyria for at least five centuries, descended from Mittani and the land of Subartu in the north-west. By the way: he apparently does not look for earlier and other lines of descent in the case of the Assyrian builders, probably Assyrians of the older stock.

Rightly Martiny points out, that the orientation of babylonian temples after 2300 b. C. badly fits the expectation of Unger about the direction of the wind, which precisely blows from that direction causing a maximum of discomfort.

Martiny searching after another explanation, thinks he finds it in astronomical motives. He states that the Assyrian temples, the later the date of the building, the more the direction of orientation turns from north to west. His arguments even try to justify a mean distancing of arc about one degree in 72,5 years, an amount which equals the precessional retrogression. He discusses the question of the Babylonian's interest in the heliacal rise of the fixed stars, the fact being of course related to the precessional cycle. Heliacal rise means the rising of a star or asterism together with the Sun and is of particular importance when the Sun rises in the exact east-point, *i. e.* at the vernal equinox, which fact consequently means the indication of the latter's place in the zodiac of the constellations. As far as the Babylonians were actually aware of the precession, they will have certainly observed it by means of heliacal rising of asterisms or sole fixed stars. Martiny has studied this matter closely and states that, of course, the heliacal stars are not visible at the day of their rising together with the Sun, but only about eleven to seventeen days afterwards, when the Sun proceeded 11—17 degrees farther. This would have been a reason for celebrating certain ritualistic festivals in honour of the stars of the vernal equinox only so many days later.

It remains vague however what this may have to do with orientation of temples. The directing on the east-point — compare Stonehenge — is well known: the direction is so as to make the Sun's rays strike an altar when rising at the vernal equinox; the cosmic year commences with the fact. Martiny reminds the fact of the procession-street at Babylon being directed at the east-point so as to make the Sun's rays at equinoxial rising fall in the direction of the street. So orientation on the Sun's rise at the vernal equinox would be stating literally what *orientation* means. This actually never appears to have been the case in Mesopotamia: the temples have been built not on the cardinal points of the compass but on the oblique cross between.

Martiny supposes the fact to be more intricate than would appear in accordance with the above evident orientation. It remains doubtful, however, whether the astronomical knowledge of the Babylonians justifies his suggestion. Principles of astrology apparently do not strengthen its footholds. The temple of Esagila for instance, devoted to Marduk-Jupiter, was orientated on the asterism Aries, says Martiny. Now Jupiter-Marduk has nothing to do with Aries, astrologically. But if Marduk as the lord of the east-point is meant, his temple ought to have been orientated *east* and not south-west. It cannot relate even to the asterism Aries being heliacal during those ages of babylonian culture; certainly not with the south-west-orientation either.

What Martiny apparently means is this: in the same way as the heliacal stars become visible only some days after their heliacal rising, the same asterisms will be visible at the easter horizon — rising before the Sun and before being obliterated by the Sun's rays — about 800 to 1200 years after their 'heliacal' ascension — to cut it short. Now this remains the east-point and for whatever other point of direction Martiny has been searching or in whatever way he may have tried to prove some or other argument for south-west or north-west has not appeared clear to me; an allusion to heliacal descent — and I am not aware that this has been ever mentioned — would have meant west exactly and not north-west or south-west.

One could also put it this way perhaps: when 700—1200 years after the heliacal rising a temple was erected as devoted to the deity of this asterism, it could have been pointed about south-eastward — there are some — but then it could never have been visually directed upon the asterism which was invisible at sunrise, blinded by the sun-rays. The changing of direction in the case of Assyrian temples is from north to west — agreeing with south to east — which is the reverse of what he actually thinks he may use as an argument: the gradually becoming visible of asterisms or stars after heliacal rise, in consequence either of the Sun's own progress (11—17 days) or of the precessional motion (700—1200 years). We let alone the fact that the Babylonians originally were more the philosophers and astrologers of the country, whereas it were the Assyrians who should have originated the said changing of temple-foundations, quite independently. In the *Zeitschrift für Assyriologie* N. F. VIII (XLII Band) A. Schott makes rather serious remarks with regard to the chronological choice of objects by Martiny in his treatise, which has not convinced me of anything at all about orientation of temples. So this remains an open question.

LITERATURE

Prof. B. Baentsch, *Altorientalischer und israelitischer Monotheismus*, Tübingen 1906 Quoted as AIM.

Carl Bezold, *Astronomie, Himmelschau und Astrallehre bei den Babyloniern*, Heidelberg 1911.

Bhagavân Dâs, *The Science of Peace*, London/Benares 1904.

H. P. Blavatsky, *The Secret Doctrine*, London/Benares 1893. Quoted as SD.

—— Translation and annotation of *The Voice of the Silence* (from the *Book of the Golden Precepts*), Peking 1927.

Prof. Dr. F. M. Th. Böhl *Kanaanäer und Hebräer*, dissertation, Leipzig 1911.

—— *Nieuwjaarsfeest en Koningsdag in Babel en Israël*, Groningen 1927.

—— Lecture to the *Vooraziatisch Egyptisch Gezelschap »Ex Oriente Lux«*, *Mededeelingen en Verhandelingen*, I, p. l, Leiden 1934.

—— *Mededeelingen uit de Leidsche Verzameling van Spijkerschrift-inscripties*, II, oorkonden uit de periode van 2000—1200 v. Chr. Mededeelingen der Kon. Akademie van Wetenschappen, afd. Letterkunde, Deel 78, Serie B. No. 2, Amsterdam 1934.

Prof. Dr. Franz Boll, *Sphaera*, neue griechische Texte und Untersuchungen zur Geschichte der Sternbilder, Leipzig 1903.

—— (mit Mitwirkung von Prof. Dr. Carl Bezold) *Sternglaube und Sterndeutung, die Geschichte und das Wesen der Astrologie*, Leipzig 1918.

A. Bouché-Leclerq, *L'Astrologie Grecque*, Paris 1899.

E. A. Wallis Budge, *The Book of the Dead*, London 1909.

Rev. E. Burgess, *Surya Siddhanta*, in *Journal of the American Oriental Society*, New Haven 1860.

Ed. Chavannes, *Le Cycle Turc des douze Animaux*, Leyden 1906.

Dr. Albert Churchward, *Signs and Symbols of Primordial Man*, London 1913.

A. Deimel, S. J. *»Enuma eliš« und Hexaëmeron*, Rome, 1934.

Friedrich Delitzsch, *Babel und Bibel*, Leipzig, Stuttgart 1905.

Dupuis, *Origine de tous les Cultes*.

Adolf Erman and Fritz Krebs, *Aus den Papyrus der Königlichen Museen*, 1899.

Prof. Dr. H. Frankfort, in his lecture to „Ex Oriente Lux", Leyden 17th May 1934, *Jaarbericht* No. 2, 1934 p. 41.

Dr. H. Girgois, *El Oculto entre los aborigenes de la America del Sad*.

Conte Goblet d'Alviella, *La Migration des Symboles*, Brussels.

Dr. Hugo Gressmann and Dr. Erich Ebeling, *Babylonisch-Assyrische Texte* in *Altorientalische Texte zum Alten Testament*, Berlin 1926.

Wilhelm Gundel, *Astronomie und Astrologie* in *Jahresbericht über die Fortschritte der Klassischen Altertumswissenschaft*, Conrad Bursian. Band 243, Jahrgang 193. Leipzig 1934.

Morris Jastrow Jr., *Die Religion Babyloniens und Assyriens*, I, II, III, Giessen 1905. British edition dates 1899. Quoted as RBA.

—— *Babylonian and Assyrian Birth-Omen* in *Religionsgeschichtliche Versuche und Vorarbeiten*. XIV, 5, Giessen 1914. Quoted as BABO.

Dr. Alfred Jeremias, *Handbuch der Altorientalischen Geisteskultur*, 2nd ed., Berlin, Leipzig 1929 Quoted as HAOG.

—— *Der Kosmos von Sumer*, Band 32, Heft 1, of the *Alte Orient* series, Leipzig 1932.

Dr. Alfred Jeremias, *Das Alter der Babylonischen Astronomie* in the series *Im Kampfe um den Alten Orient.*

Johannes Kepler, *Tertius Interveniens.* Compare *Johannes Keplers Kosmische Harmonie,* herausgegeben und übertragen von W. Harburger, Leipzig 1925.

Prof. E. Kern *Brihat Samhita* and *Brihat Jakata, in the Journal of the Royal Asiatic Soc. of Great Britain and Ireland,* London 1870/75.

L. W. King, *History of Sumer and Akkad.*

—— *The Seven Tablets of Creation,* 1902.

Friedrich Kirchner, *Wörterbuch der Philosophischen Grundbegriffe,* 5th ed., Leipzig 1907.

Dr. Martin Knapp, *Antiskia, Ein Beitrag zum Wissen um die Präzession im Altertum,* Basel 1927.

Felix X. Kugler S. J., *Sternkunde und Sterndienst in Babel,* Münster i/W., 1907/'24. Quoted as SSB.

—— *Im Bannkreis Babels,* Münster i/W. 1910. Quoted as IBB.

—— *Zur Aufklärnng — Ueber die Sternenfahrt des Gilgamesch.*

B. Landsberger, *Babylonisch-Assyrische Texte* in *Textbuch für Religionsgeschichte,* 1922.

S. Langdon, *The Babylonian Epic of Creation,* Oxford 1923. Quoted as BEC.

Troels Lund, *Himmelsbild und Weltanschauung im Wandel der Zeiten,* 3rd ed., Leipzig 1908.

Günther Martiny, *Die Kultrichtung in Mesopotamien,* dissertation, Berlin 1932.

Bruno Meissner, *Babylonien und Assyrien* I and II, Heidelberg 1920 and 1925. Quoted as BA.

Prof. C. Schlegel, *Uranographie Chinoise,* Leyden 1874.

A. Schott, in *Zeitschrift für Assyriologie,* N. F. VIII (Band XLII).

Dr. A. van Selms, at the congress of the *Oostersch Genootschap in Nederland,* September 1933 at Leyden, published in the *Mededeelingen en Verhandelingen* No. 1 of the *Voor-Aziatisch Egyptisch Gezelschap »Ex Oriente Lux«,* Leyden 1934.

Dr. Ludwig Staudenmaier, *Die Magie als experimentelle Naturwissenschaft,* Leipzig 1912.

Rabindranath Tagore, *Gitanjali* (*Song Offerings*), London 1913.

A. E. Thierens, *Natural Philosophy,* London 1928. Quoted as N. Ph.

—— *The General Book of the Tarot,* London 1928. Quoted as GBT.

—— *Elements of Esoteric Astrology,* London 1931. Quoted as EEA.

R. Campbell Thompson. *The Reports of the Magicians and Astrologers of Nineveh and Babylon in the British Museum,* London 1900. Quoted as *Reports.*

F. Thureau Dangin, *Textes Cunéiformes du Musée du Louvre,* Tôme 6, Planche 27—28.

Eckhard Unger, *Babylon, die Heilige Stadt,* Berlin Leipzig 1931. Quoted as *Babylon.*

Arthur Ungnad, *Die Religion der Babylonier und Assyrier,* Jena 1921. Quoted as RBAU.

Ch. Virolleaud, *l'Astrologie Chaldéenne, Paris* 1903/1912.

Ernst F. Weidner, *Handbuch der Babylonischen Astronomie*; *Assyriologische Bibliothek XXIII,* Leipzig 1915 Quoted as. HBA.

Hugo Winckler, *Im Kampfe um den Alten Orient,* Leipzig 1907—1914.

Herman Wirth, *Aufgang der Menschheit.*

Gundel's instalment in Bursian's is extremely usefull and contains a pretty complete information on this subject.

LIST OF ABBREVIATIONS

AIM.	Baentsch, *Altorientalischer und Israelitischer Monotheismus,* Tübingen 1906.
BA.	Meissner, *Babylonien und Assyrien,* Heidelberg 1925.
BABO.	Jastrow, *Babylonian and Assyrian Birth-Omen* in *Religionsgeschichtliche Versuche und Vorarbeiten,* XIV, 5, Giessen 1914.
Babylon	Unger, *Babylon, die Heilige Stadt,* Berlin-Leipzig 1931.
BEC.	Langdon, *The Babylonian Epic of Creation,* Oxford 1923.

EEA.	Thierens, *Elements of Esoteric Astrology*, London 1931.
GBT.	Thierens, *The General Book of te Tarot*, London 1928.
HAOG.	Jeremias, *Handbuch der Altorientalischen Geisteskultur*, 2 nd, ed. Berlin, Leipzig 1929.
HBA.	Weidner, *Handbuch der Babylonischen Astronomie, Assyriologische Bibliothek* XXIII, Leipzig 1915.
IBB.	Kugler, *Im Bannkreis Babels*, Münster i.W. 1910.
N. Ph.	Thierens, *Natural Philosophy*, London 1928.
RBA.	Jastrow, *Die Religion Babyloniens und Assyriens*, I, II, III, Giessen 1905.
RBAU.	Ungnad, *Die Religion der Babylonier und Assyrier*, Jena 1921.
Reports	Thompson, *The Reports of the Magicians and Astrologers of Nineveh and Babylon iu the British Museum*, London 1900.
SD.	Blavatsky, *The Secret Doctrine*, London/Benares 1893.
SSB.	Kugler, *Sternkunde und Sterndienst in Babel*, Münster i/W., 1907—1924.

www.ingramcontent.com/pod-product-compliance
Lightning Source LLC
LaVergne TN
LVHW080248110826
845148LV00023BA/873

* 9 7 8 1 7 2 5 2 7 9 3 0 8 *